THE SHADOW

*Evgeny Shvarts
Translated from the
Russian by
Laurence Senelick*

BROADWAY PLAY PUBLISHING INC
New York
www.broadwayplaypub.com
info@broadwayplaypub.com

Cover art by Nikolai Akimov for the poster for the first production of the play

First edition: April 2019
I S B N: 978-0-88145-840-4

Book design: Marie Donovan
Page make-up: Adobe InDesign
Typeface: Palatino

THE SHADOW was first performed at the Comedy Theatre, Leningrad, 1940.

CHARACTERS

THE SCHOLAR
HIS SHADOW
PIETRO, AN INNKEEPER
ANNUNCIATA, HIS DAUGHTER
GIULIA GIULI, A SINGER
THE PRINCESS
PRIME MINISTER
FINANCE MINISTER
CESARE BORGIA, A JOURNALIST
PRIVY COUNCILOR
DOCTOR
HEADSMAN
MAJOR-DOMO
CORPORAL
LADIES OF THE COURT
COURTIERS
SPA-GOERS
SISTER OF MIRTH
SISTER OF MERCY
ROYAL HERALDS
LACKEYS OF THE FINANCE MINISTER
GUARDS
TOWNSFOLK

...And the scholar grew angry not only because the shadow had left him, but more because he remembered the famous story about the man without a shadow, which each and every one in his native land knew. Now were he to go back home and tell his story, everyone would say that he had taken to imitating others...

Hans Christian Andersen, *The Shadow*

...Someone else's story seems to have burrowed so deep into my flesh and blood that I recreated it and only then released it into the world.

Hans Christian Andersen, *The Fairy-tale of My Life*, chapter 8

ACT ONE

(A small room in an inn in a southern land. Two doors: one to the corridor, the other to the balcony. Semi-recumbent on a sofa lies the SCHOLAR, *a young man of twenty. His hand is fumbling on the table—looking for his eye-glasses.)*

SCHOLAR: When you misplace your eye-glasses, it's a nuisance, of course. But then again it's delightful—in the twilight my whole room looks quite unlike its usual self. This lap rug, tossed on an armchair, now appears to be a very sweet and gentle princess. I am in love with her, and she has paid me a call. She's not alone, of course. A princess is not supposed to go around without an escort. That tall, narrow clock in its wooden case is not a clock at all. It is the princess's constant companion, the Privy Councilor. His heart beats regularly like a pendulum, his counsel changes to suit the demands of the time, and he offers it in a whisper. There's a good reason he's called privy. And if the Privy Councilor's counsel turns out to be disastrous, he will therefore distance himself from it completely. He will insist that people didn't catch what he said, and this is very practical on his part. And who is that? Who is that uncanny figure, slender and shapely, all in black, with the chalky face? Why does it suddenly occur to me that it may be the Princess's fiancé? After all, I'm the one in love with the Princess! I'm so in love with her that it would be perfectly monstrous if she were to marry someone else. *(Laughs)* The charm of all these fantasies lies in the fact that as soon as I put on my glasses, everything will fall back into place. *The lap rug will become a lap rug, the clock a clock, and that sinister stranger will disappear.* (*His hands fumble on the table with his hands.*) Here are my glasses. (*Puts on his glasses and cries out*) What's this?

(*In the armchair sits a very beautiful, luxuriously dressed* YOUNG LADY IN A MASK. *Behind her a bald* OLD MAN IN A FROCKCOAT WITH A STAR *on his chest. And clinging to the wall is a lanky, gaunt, pale* MAN IN A BLACK TAILCOAT *and dazzling linen. On his finger a diamond signet-ring.*)

SCHOLAR: (*Mutters, lighting a candle.*) What kind of wonder is this? I'm a humble scholar—how do I rate such important guests? ...Good evening, my friends! I'm pleased to see you, my friends, but... might you explain to what do I owe such an honor? You keep silent? Ah, I get it. I dozed off. It's a dream.

YOUNG LADY IN A MASK: No, it's not a dream.

SCHOLAR: Really! Then what is it?

YOUNG LADY IN A MASK: It's just a fairy tale. Good-bye, Mister Scholar! We shall meet again.

MAN IN TAIL COAT: Good-bye, scholar! We shall meet again.

OLD MAN WITH STAR: (*In a whisper*) Good-bye, respected scholar! We shall meet again, and everything may, perhaps, end happily ever after, if you behave sensibly.

(*Knock on the door, all three vanish.*)

SCHOLAR: What a story!

(*The knock is repeated.*)

SCHOLAR: Come in!

(ANNUNCIATA *enters the room, a black-haired young woman with big black eyes. Her face is extremely mobile, but her manners and voice are gentle and hesitant. She is very beautiful. About seventeen*)

ANNUNCIATA: Excuse me, sir, you have guests... Ah!

SCHOLAR: What's wrong, Annunciata?

ANNUNCIATA: But I clearly heard voices in your room!

SCHOLAR: I dozed off and was talking in my sleep.

ANNUNCIATA: But...excuse me...I heard a woman's voice.

SCHOLAR: I was dreaming about a princess.

ANNUNCIATA: And some old man was muttering something under his breath.

SCHOLAR: I was dreaming about a Privy Councilor.

ANNUNCIATA: And some other man, so it seemed, was shouting at you.

SCHOLAR: That was the princess's fiancé. Well? Now do you see it was a dream? If I were awake, would I entertain such unpleasant guests?

ANNUNCIATA: Are you joking?

SCHOLAR: Yes.

ANNUNCIATA: Thank you for that. You're always so kind to me. I probably heard voices in the next room and got confused. But...you won't be angry? May I tell you something?

SCHOLAR: Of course, Annunciata.

ANNUNCIATA: I've been wanting to warn you for a long time. Don't be angry... You're a scholar, and I'm a simple girl. And yet...I can tell you something that I know and you don't. (*Curtsies*) Excuse my boldness.

SCHOLAR: Please! Speak out! Inform me! I may be a scholar, but scholars go on learning all the time.

ANNUNCIATA: Are you joking?

SCHOLAR: No, I'm completely serious.

ANNUNCIATA: Thank you for that. *(Glancing at the door)* In books about our country they always write about the wholesome climate, the clean air, the beautiful views, the hot sun, well…in short, you know yourself what is written in books about our country…

SCHOLAR: Of course I know. That's why I came here.

ANNUNCIATA: Yes. You know what's written about us in books, but what isn't written about us in them you don't know.

SCHOLAR: That's not uncommon with scholars.

ANNUNCIATA: You don't know that you are living in a very special country. Everything that's told in fairy tales, everything that in other lands seems like fantasy—actually happens every day. For instance, Sleeping Beauty lived five hours' walk from the tobacconist's—the one to the right of the fountain. Only Sleeping Beauty is dead now. The man-eating Ogre is still alive and works as an appraiser in the municipal pawnshop. Hop o' My Thumb married a very tall woman, nicknamed Grenadier, and their children are of normal height, same as you or me. And you know what's wonderful about it? This woman, nicknamed Grenadier, is completely under Hop o' My Thumb's thumb. She even takes him to market with her. Hop o' My Thumb sits in the pocket of her apron and bargains like the very devil. And yet they live together very affectionately. The wife is so attentive to her husband. Every time they dance a minuet on holidays, she wears bifocals so as not to step on her spouse accidentally.

SCHOLAR: That is very interesting indeed, why don't they write about this in books about your country?

ANNUNCIATA: *(Glancing at the door.)* Not everybody likes fairy tales.

SCHOLAR: Really?

ANNUNCIATA: Yes, can you imagine! *(Glancing at the door.)* We're awfully worried that if this got out, people would stop coming here. It would be so bad for the economy! Don't give us away, please.

SCHOLAR: No, I won't tell a soul.

ANNUNCIATA: Thank you for that. My poor father loves money, and I'd be upset if he starts to earn less than he counts on. When he's out of sorts, he swears a blue streak!

SCHOLAR: And yet I expect the number of tourists would increase if they knew that in your country fairy tales come true.

ANNUNCIATA: No. If children visited us, it might be so. But grown-ups are a cautious race. They know perfectly well that many fairy tales have unhappy endings. That's what I wanted to talk to you about. Be careful.

SCHOLAR: What of? To avoid catching a cold you have to dress warmly. To avoid stumbling you have to look where you're going. But how do you avoid fairy tales with unhappy endings?

ANNUNCIATA: Well…I don't know… You mustn't talk to people you don't know very well.

SCHOLAR: Then I'd have to keep silent all the time. After all I'm a newcomer here.

ANNUNCIATA: No, honestly, please be careful. You are a very nice man, and those are the ones who most often come to a bad end.

SCHOLAR: How do know I'm a nice man?

ANNUNCIATA: I hang out in the kitchen a lot. Our cook has eleven lady friends. And they all know everything that is, was, and is to come. Nothing is hidden from them. They know what goes on in every family, as if the house had glass walls. In the kitchen we laugh and cry and scare each other. On days when things get especially interesting whatever's on the stove gets overcooked. They are unanimous in saying you are a fine man.

SCHOLAR: Were they the ones who told you that in your country fairy tales come true?

ANNUNCIATA: Yes.

SCHOLAR: You know, in the evening, especially when I take off my glasses, I'm ready to believe it. But in the morning, leaving the house, I see things quite differently. Your country—alas!—is like any other country on earth. Wealth and poverty, celebrity and slavery, death and disaster, intelligence and stupidity, holiness, crime, conscience, shamelessness—it's all mixed up so randomly it simply gives you the willies. It would be no easy task to sort it out, organize and arrange things so that no living creature gets harmed. Things are much simpler in fairy tales.

ANNUNCIATA: *(Bobbing)* Thank you very much.

SCHOLAR: What for?

ANNUNCIATA: For speaking so eloquently to me, a simple girl.

SCHOLAR: Don't mention it. We scholars are like that. But tell me, my friend Hans Christian Andersen, who once lived in this room before I did, did he know about the fairy tales?

ANNUNCIATA: Yes, somehow he found out about them.

SCHOLAR: And what did he say to that?

ANNUNCIATA: He said: "All my life I've suspected
I've been writing the truth." He was very fond of our
house. He liked that it was so quiet here.

(A deafening gunshot)

SCHOLAR: What's that?

ANNUNCIATA: Oh, pay it no mind. It's my father at
odds with somebody or other. He's very hot-tempered
and fires a pistol at the drop of a hat. But so far he
hasn't killed anyone. He's nervous—and that's why he
always misses.

SCHOLAR: I understand. I'm familiar with that
phenomenon. If he ever hit the target, he wouldn't fire
so often.

PIETRO: *(A bellow offstage:)* Annunciata!

ANNUNCIATA: *(Meekly)* Coming, daddykins darlin'.
Good-bye! Ah, I quite forgot why I came. Which do
you prefer—coffee or milk?

*(The door bursts open with a crash. Into the room runs
a well-built, broad-shouldered, youthful looking man.
He resembles* ANNUNCIATA. *Surly, won't look anyone
in the face. He is the landlord of the furnished rooms,*
ANNUNCIATA's *father,* PIETRO.*)*

PIETRO: Why don't you come when you're called?!
Go at once and reload my pistol. She bound to have
heard—her father's shootin'. Gotta explain everything,
gotta stick their nose in everywhere. I'll kill 'em!

*(*ANNUNCIATA *calmly and boldly steps up to* PIETRO, *kisses
his brow.)*

ANNUNCIATA: I'm going, daddykins. Good-bye, sir!
(Exits)

SCHOLAR: As you can see, your daughter is not afraid
of you, Signor Pietro.

PIETRO: No, stab me vitals. She treats me as if I was the most doting father in town.

SCHOLAR: Maybe you are?

PIETRO: 'S not her business to know. I can't stand it when people try to figger out what I'm thinkin' and feelin'. Nothin' but pains in the neck all round. The lodger in room fifteen just now refused to pay again. In my rage I shot at the lodger in room fourteen.

SCHOLAR: Didn't he pay either?

PIETRO: He did. But fourteen's a nobody. Our Prime Minister can't stand 'im. But the other one, that damned non-payer, fifteen, works on our super-nasty newspaper. Oh, let the whole world go to hell in a hand-basket! I twist and turn like a corkscrew to squeeze money out of the lodgers in my miserable inn and can't make ends meet. What's more, I gotta work a gummint job, so's not to starve to death.

SCHOLAR: You really have a government job?

PIETRO: Yes.

SCHOLAR: Where?

PIETRO: Appraiser at the municipal pawnshop.

(Music suddenly begins to play—barely audible sometimes, sometimes as if it's playing right in the room.)

SCHOLAR: Tell… Tell me… Tell me please, where's that coming from?

PIETRO: Across the way.

SCHOLAR: And who lives there?

PIETRO: I dunno. They say some flippin' princess.

SCHOLAR: A princess?

PIETRO: So they say. I came here on business. That damn number fifteen asks you to see him. This

newspaper boyo. This thief who's aimin' to live for free
in a de-luxe room. May I?

SCHOLAR: Please. I'd be delighted.

PIETRO: Don't be delighted before the time comes.
Good-bye! *(Exits)*

SCHOLAR: This innkeeper is an appraiser in the
municipal pawnshop. A man-eating ogre? Just
imagine!

(The SCHOLAR *opens the door to the balcony. The wall of
the house across the way is visible. The street is narrow.
The balcony of the house across the way touches the balcony
of his room. He has barely opened the door when the street
noise bursts through the window. Individual voices can be
made out from the general din.)*

VOICES:

Watermelons, watermelons! By the slice!

Water, water, ice-cold water!

Here they are—knives for killing! Who wants a
knife for killing?!

Flowers, flowers! Roses! Lilies! Tulips!

Make way for the donkey, make way for the
donkey! Step aside, people: here comes the donkey!

Alms for a poor mute!

Poisons, poisons, fresh-made poisons!

SCHOLAR: Our street is seething like a regular cauldron.
I really like it here! ...If it weren't for my constant
restlessness, if I didn't think the whole world is
unhappy because I haven't yet come up with a way to
save it, things would be quite pleasant. And when the
young lady who lives across the way comes out on her
balcony, I feel as if there's just one thing I have to do,

just one little effort I have to make—and it will all fall into place.

(Into the SCHOLAR'*s room comes a very beautiful young* WOMAN, *elegantly dressed. She squints, glances around. He does not notice her.)*

SCHOLAR: If harmony prevails in the sea, the mountains, the forest and in oneself, that means the world is constructed more intelligently than...

WOMAN: That won't do.

SCHOLAR: *(Turns around.)* Excuse me!

WOMAN: No, it won't. What you've been muttering doesn't possess a shadow of wit. Is this your new column? Where are you? How are you today? Don't you recognize me or what?

SCHOLAR: Forgive me, no.

WOMAN: Stop teasing me for being near-sighted. It's impolite. Where are you?

SCHOLAR: I'm here.

WOMAN: Come closer.

SCHOLAR: Here I am. *(Steps up to the stranger)*

WOMAN: *(She is genuinely surprised.)* Who are you?

SCHOLAR: I'm a traveller, I am living at the inn. That's who I am.

WOMAN: Forgive me... My eyes have misled me again. Isn't this room fifteen?

SCHOLAR: No, unfortunately.

WOMAN: What a kind and handsome face you have! Why haven't you been to our club before now, our club of real people?

SCHOLAR: What kind of club is it?

WOMAN: Oh, performers, writers, courtiers. Even a cabinet minister drops in. We are the fashionistas, devoid of prejudice, and we understand everything. Are you famous?

SCHOLAR: No.

WOMAN: What a pity! That's not acceptable. But... but I think I'm prepared to forgive you that... seeing as how I've suddenly taken a liking to you. Are you angry with me?

SCHOLAR: No, what for!

WOMAN: I'll sit with you a while. May I?

SCHOLAR: Of course.

WOMAN: It has suddenly occurred to me that you are just the man I've been looking for all my life. Ordinarily, you get the impression—from his voice and his way of speaking—that there's the very man, but whenever he comes a bit closer, you can see he isn't Mr Right at all. But it's too late to retreat, he has come too close. It's a dreadful thing to be beautiful and nearsighted. Am I boring you?

SCHOLAR: No, of course not!

WOMAN: How simply and calmly you make your replies! And he gets on my nerves.

SCHOLAR: Who?

WOMAN: The man I came here to see. He is dreadfully restless. He wants to please everyone in the world. He's a slave of fashion. For instance, when it was fashionable to have a sun-tan, he got so tanned he turned black as an African. And then tanning suddenly went out of fashion. And he decided to have an operation. Skin from under his swimming-trunks— that was the only white spot on his body—the doctors grafted on to his face.

SCHOLAR: I hope it didn't hurt him?

WOMAN: No. He only became remarkably shameless and now he simply considers a slap in the face a spanking.

SCHOLAR: Why are you calling on him?

WOMAN: Well, all the same this man is a member of our club, the club of real people. Besides, he works on the newspaper. You know who I am?

SCHOLAR: No.

WOMAN: I am a singer. My name is Giulia Giuli.

SCHOLAR: You're very famous in this country!

GIULIA: Yes. Everyone knows my songs *Mama, What is This Thing Called Love?*, *Girls, Haste to Find Happiness, My Lover's Heartbreak Leaves Me Cold* and *Ah, Why Am I Not a Forest Glade?* Are you a doctor?

SCHOLAR: No, a PhD in History.

GIULIA: You're vacationing here?

SCHOLAR: I'm studying the history of your country.

GIULIA: Our country is so small.

SCHOLAR: Yes, but its history is like all the others. And that makes me happy.

GIULIA: Why?

SCHOLAR: It means that the earth is governed by laws valid for everyone. When you live in one place for a long time, in one and the same room and you see one and the same people, whom you chose as friends, the world seems very simple. But you're barely out the door and—there's far too much variety. And this…

(Someone cries out in alarm behind the door. Sound of glass breaking)

SCHOLAR: Who's there?

An elegant YOUNG MAN *enters, shaking himself off. A
distraught* ANNUNCIATA *is behind him.*

YOUNG MAN: Good evening! I was standing by your
door, and frightened Annunciata. Am I really so
terrifying?

ANNUNCIATA: *(To the* SCHOLAR*)* Sorry, I dropped the
glass of milk I was bringing you.

YOUNG MAN: And you don't ask my pardon?

ANNUNCIATA: But it's all your fault, sir! Why were you
lurking at someone else's door, standing there without
moving?

YOUNG MAN: I was eavesdropping. *(To the* SCHOLAR*)*
Do you like my frankness? All scholars are
straightforward people. You ought to like it. Do you?
Well, tell me whether you like my frankness. Did you
like me?

GIULIA: Don't answer him. If you say "yes", he will
despise you, but if you say "no", he will start to hate
you.

YOUNG MAN: Giulia, Giulia, malicious Giulia! *(To
the* SCHOLAR*)* Allow me to introduce myself: Cesare
Borgia. You've heard of me?

SCHOLAR: Yes.

CESARE BORGIA: Really? Is that so? What exactly have
you heard of me?

SCHOLAR: Plenty.

CESARE BORGIA: Did they praise me? Or insult me?
And who precisely?

SCHOLAR: I've simply read your critical and political
articles in the local paper.

CESARE BORGIA: They enjoy a certain popularity. But
someone is always dissatisfied. You malign a man, and

he's dissatisfied. I would like to discover the secret of total popularity. To find that secret I'm capable of anything. Do you like my frankness?

GIULIA: Let's go. We've intruded on the Scholar, and scholars are constantly busy.

CESARE BORGIA: I warned Mister Scholar in advance. Our innkeeper told him that I'd be coming. And you, my gorgeous Giulia, did you mistake the room?

GIULIA: No, I think I came just when I was supposed to.

CESARE BORGIA: But you were coming to see *me*! I just finished an article about you. You'll like it, but—alas!— your lady friends will not. *(To the* SCHOLAR*)* You will allow us to call on you later today?

SCHOLAR: Please do.

CESARE BORGIA: I want to write an article about you.

SCHOLAR: Thanks. It may be useful for my work in your archives. It will give me more prestige.

CESARE BORGIA: Clever fellow! Actually I know why you came here. Your business here is not in the archives.

SCHOLAR: What is it then?

CESARE BORGIA: Clever fellow! You keep staring at the balcony across the way.

SCHOLAR: Do I really stare at it?

CESARE BORGIA: Yes you do. You think that's where she lives.

SCHOLAR: Who?

CESARE BORGIA: You don't have to be so secretive. After all you're an historian, you're studying our country. Consequently you know of the will and testament of our last king, Louis the Ninth, the Daydreamer.

SCHOLAR: Excuse me, but I've only made it to the end of the sixteenth century.

CESARE BORGIA: Is that so? And you know nothing of the will and testament?

SCHOLAR: I assure you I do not.

CESARE BORGIA: Strange. Then why did you ask the innkeeper to assign you this very room?

SCHOLAR: Because my friend Hans Christian Andersen lived here once.

CESARE BORGIA: Is that the only reason?

SCHOLAR: I give you my word it is. And what connection is there between my room and the late king's will?

CESARE BORGIA: Oh, a very great deal. Good-bye! May I escort you, fascinating Giulia?

SCHOLAR: May I ask just what was in this mysterious will and testament?

CESARE BORGIA: Oh no, I'm not talking. I have an interest in it myself. I want power, respect, and I have a terrible want of money. That I, Cesare Borgia, whose name is known throughout the land, has to work as a simple appraiser in the municipal pawnshop. Do you like my frankness?

GIULIA: Let's go! Let's go! Everyone likes you. He never just leaves. (To the SCHOLAR) We shall meet again.

SCHOLAR: I'll be delighted.

CESARE BORGIA: Don't be delighted before the time comes!

(CESARE BORGIA and GIULIA exit.)

SCHOLAR: Annunciata, how many appraisers are there in your municipal pawnshop?

ANNUNCIATA: Lots.

SCHOLAR: And are they all ex-ogres?

ANNUNCIATA: Almost all.

SCHOLAR: What's wrong with you? Why are you so downcast?

ANNUNCIATA: Ah, didn't I ask you to be careful! People say that this singer Giulia Giuli was the same little girl who trampled on a loaf of bread to keep her new shoes clean.

SCHOLAR: But, as I recall, that little girl was punished for it.

ANNUNCIATA: Yes, she fell through the earth, but then she scrambled out again and from that time on keeps on trampling, trampling on good people, on her best friends, even on herself—and all to keep her new shoes, stockings and dresses clean. Now I'll bring you another glass of milk.

SCHOLAR: Hold on! I don't want a drink, I want to talk to you.

ANNUNCIATA: Thank you for that.

SCHOLAR: Please tell me about the will left by the late king Louis the Ninth the Daydreamer.

ANNUNCIATA: Oh, that's a secret, a solemn secret! The will was sealed inside seven envelopes with seven waxen seals and countersigned by seven Privy Councilors. The Princess was completely alone when she opened it and read it. Guards stood at the windows and doors, their ears plugged just in case, although the princess was reading the will to herself. What was written in that secret document is known only to the princess and the whole town.

SCHOLAR: The whole town?

ANNUNCIATA: Yes.

SCHOLAR: How did that happen?

ANNUNCIATA: No one can explain it. It would appear that every precaution was taken. It's simply a miracle. Everyone knows the will. Even the ragamuffins in the street.

SCHOLAR: What is written in it?

ANNUNCIATA: Ah, don't ask me.

SCHOLAR: Why not?

ANNUNCIATA: I very much fear that this will and testament is the beginning of a new fairy tale, which will have an unhappy ending.

SCHOLAR: Annunciata, I'm just passing through, am I not? Your king's will has nothing to do with me. Tell me. Otherwise things might go badly: I'm a scholar, an historian—and yet I don't know what every ragamuffin in the street knows! Please tell me.

ANNUNCIATA: *(Sighing)* All right, here goes. When a good man asks me, I can refuse him nothing. Our cook says it will get me into serious trouble. But let the trouble fall on my head, not yours. Anyway... Are you listening?

SCHOLAR: What do you think!

ANNUNCIATA: Then why are you staring at the balcony across the way?

SCHOLAR: No, no... You see, I'm settling in comfortably, I'm puffing on my pipe, and I won't take my eyes off your face.

ANNUNCIATA: Thank you. Anyway, five years ago our king Louis the Ninth the Daydreamer died. The ragamuffins in the street didn't call him the Daydreamer, but the Dummy, but that wasn't right. The deceased, true, often leaned out the window and stuck out his tongue at them, but it was the ragamuffins' own fault. Why did they tease him? The deceased was a clever man, but such are the duties of a king that it spoiled his temper. At the very start of his reign the Prime Minister, whom the sovereign trusted more than his own father, poisoned the king's favorite sister. The king executed the Prime Minister. The second Prime Minister was not a poisoner, but he lied so much that the king stopped believing anyone, even himself. The third Prime Minister was not a liar, but he was dreadfully cunning. He wove and wove and wove the subtlest webs around the simplest matters. The king in his last proclamation wanted to say "I declare" and suddenly he was buzzing faintly like a fly caught in a spider web. So the minister flew away at the insistence of the king's physician in ordinary. The fourth Prime Minister was not a sly boots. He was upright and simple. He stole the king's gold snuffbox and ran away. And the sovereign turned his back on affairs of state. From that time on the Prime Ministers began to name their own replacements. And the sovereign went in for theatre. But they say this was even worse than running a kingdom. After a year's work in the theatre the king began to freeze.

SCHOLAR: What do you mean freeze?

ANNUNCIATA: Plain and simple. He'd be walking along—and suddenly he'd go stiff, with one leg in the air. And his face would freeze in an expression of despair. The physician in ordinary explained that it was because the king got incurably confused, trying to figure out what connection workers in the theatre had to each other. After all, there are so many of them!

SCHOLAR: The physician in ordinary was right.

ANNUNCIATA: He prescribed a simple treatment, which no doubt would have cured the poor king. He prescribed executing half the company, but the king wouldn't agree.

SCHOLAR: Why not?

ANNUNCIATA: He could never decide exactly which half deserved execution. And finally the king turned his back on it all and began to run after women of ill repute, and they were the only ones who didn't deceive him.

SCHOLAR: Really?

ANNUNCIATA: Yes, yes! For they were genuinely women of ill repute. That is, exactly what people said they were. And this greatly comforted the king, but finally undermined his health. And his legs became paralyzed. And from that time on they began to push him about the palace in a wheelchair, while he kept silent and thought and thought and thought. What he thought about he never told anyone. Every so often the sovereign would order them to wheel him to a window and, opening a pane, he would stick out his tongue at the ragamuffins in the street, who jumped and shouted, "Dummy, dummy, dummy!" And then the king drew up his will. And then he died.

SCHOLAR: We've finally come to the heart of the matter.

ANNUNCIATA: When the king died, his only daughter, the princess, was thirteen years old. "Dearest," he said to her in his will, "I have lived my life badly, have done nothing with it. You have done nothing either—you are being poisoned by the air in the palace. I do not want you to marry a prince. I know every single one of the princes in the world. They are far too stupid for such a little country as ours. When you have reached the age of eighteen, settle somewhere in town and search, search, search. Find yourself a good, honest, educated, intelligent husband. Even if he's a commoner. And just suppose if he manages to do what none of the nobility has been able to do? Just suppose if he will know how to rule and rule well? Eh? Wouldn't that be nice! So please try hard, Papa."

SCHOLAR: That's what he wrote?

ANNUNCIATA: Exactly. The will has been recited so many times in the kitchen that I memorized it word for word.

SCHOLAR: And now the princess is living in town?

ANNUNCIATA: Yes. But it's not so easy to find her.

SCHOLAR: Why is that?

ANNUNCIATA: Scads of women of ill repute have rented whole floors of houses and pretend to be princesses.

SCHOLAR: But you know the princess by sight?

ANNUNCIATA: No. After she read the will, the Princess took to wearing a mask so that no one could recognize her when she set out to find a husband.

SCHOLAR: Tell me, she… *(Falls silent)*

(On the balcony across the way a YOUNG LADY *with fair hair enters, in a modest dark dress.)*

SCHOLAR: Tell me, she… What was I going to ask you?.. However…no, not about that.

ANNUNCIATA: You're not looking at me again?

SCHOLAR: I'm not? …Then where am I looking?

ANNUNCIATA: Over there… Ah! Let me close the door to the balcony.

SCHOLAR: What for? Don't! It's only just beginning to cool off.

ANNUNCIATA: After sundown it's best to shut the windows and doors. Otherwise you can catch malaria. No, malaria has nothing to do with it! You mustn't look over there. Please… Are you mad at me? Don't be angry… Don't look at that girl. Let me close the door to the balcony. You're just like a little child, aren't you. You won't eat your soup, but without soup there's no supper! You send your linen to the laundry without a list. And with the same good-natured, cheerful face you walk straight into the jaws of death. I'm speaking so boldly that I 've lost track of what I'm saying: it's insolent, but you have to be warned. They say that this young lady is a woman of ill repute... Stop, stop... So far as I'm concerned, that's not so awful... I'm afraid the matter is much worse.

SCHOLAR: You think so?

ANNUNCIATA: Yes. And what if this young lady turns out to be the princess? What then? What will you do then?

SCHOLAR: Of course, of course.

ANNUNCIATA: Are you listening to what I'm saying?

SCHOLAR: Sure I am!

ANNUNCIATA: After all, if she's really the princess, everyone will want to marry her and you'll be trampled in the stampede.

SCHOLAR: Yes, yes, of course.

ANNUNCIATA: No, I can see there's nothing I can do about it. I'm such an unhappy girl, sir.

SCHOLAR: True enough.

(ANNUNCIATA goes to the door to the corridor. The SCHOLAR goes to the door that leads to the balcony. She glances around. She stops in place.)

ANNUNCIATA: Good-bye, sir. (Quietly, with surprising energy.) I won't let anyone hurt you. Not for the world. Never. (Exits.)

(The SCHOLAR looks at the YOUNG LADY standing on the balcony across the way, she is looking down at the street. He begins to speak quietly, then gradually more loudly. By the

*end of his monologue she is looking at him, not taking her
eyes off him.)*

SCHOLAR: Of course, the world is organized more
intelligently than it would appear. A little longer—two
or three days' work—and I shall understand how to
make everyone happy. Everyone will be happy, but
not as much as I am. It's only here in the evenings,
when you come out on the balcony that I began to
understand that I can be happier than anyone else. I
know you, —how can one not know you? I understand
you the way I understand good weather, the moon,
a mountain pass. After all, it's so simple. I cannot say
exactly what you're thinking, but on the other hand I
do know exactly that your thoughts would cheer me as
much as your face, your braid and eyelashes do. Thank
you for it all: for choosing this house, for being born
and living at the same time I am. What would I have
done, had I not met you! Strange to think of!

YOUNG LADY: Did you recite that by heart?

SCHOLAR: I…I…

YOUNG LADY: Do go on.

SCHOLAR: You're talking to me!

YOUNG LADY: Did you make it up all by yourself or did
you commission it from somebody?

SCHOLAR: Forgive me, but your voice so staggers me
that I don't understand a word.

YOUNG LADY: You rather deftly avoided giving a direct
answer. I suppose what you said to me you made up
by yourself. Or maybe not. Well, all right, we'll drop it.
I'm bored today. How do you have the patience to sit
in the same room all day long? This closet?

SCHOLAR: Excuse me?

YOUNG LADY: This closet or wardrobe or parlor or one of the antechambers?

SCHOLAR: It's simply my room. My one and only room.

YOUNG LADY: You're a pauper?

SCHOLAR: No, I'm a scholar.

YOUNG LADY: If you say so. You have a very odd face.

SCHOLAR: How so?

YOUNG LADY: When you talk, it seems as if you're not lying.

SCHOLAR: In fact I am not lying.

YOUNG LADY: Everyone is a liar.

SCHOLAR: That's not true.

YOUNG LADY: No, it is true. Perhaps they don't lie to you—you've got only one room, —but they lie to me all the time. It makes me sorry for myself.

SCHOLAR: What are you saying? They insult you? Who does?

YOUNG LADY: You so deftly pretend to be attentive and kindly that I should like to complain to you.

SCHOLAR: You're that unhappy?

YOUNG LADY: I don't know. Yes.

SCHOLAR: Why?

YOUNG LADY: No special reason. Everyone is a scoundrel.

SCHOLAR: You mustn't talk like that. The people who talk like that are the ones who've taken the most horrible path in life. They ruthlessly smother, trample, steal, slander: how can you be sorry for anyone if everyone's a scoundrel!

YOUNG LADY: So, in other words, not everyone is?

SCHOLAR: Not at all.

YOUNG LADY: Good, if only it were true. I'm terribly worried about turning into a frog.

SCHOLAR: A frog?

YOUNG LADY: You've heard the fairy tale about the frog princess? They tell it wrong. In fact it was all quite different. I know this for a fact. The frog princess is my cousin.

SCHOLAR: Your cousin?

YOUNG LADY: Yes. Once removed. The story goes that the frog princess kissed a man who fell in love with her, despite her unsightly exterior. And that made the frog turn into a beautiful woman. Right?

SCHOLAR: So far as I can recall.

YOUNG LADY: In fact my cousin was a beautiful maiden, and she married a scoundrel, who only pretended to love her. And his kisses were so cold and repulsive that the beautiful maiden turned in no time into a cold and repulsive frog. This was very unpleasant for us, her family. They say such things happen much more often than one might think. Only my cousin didn't bother to conceal her transformation. She was extremely uninhibited. It's awful. Am I right?

SCHOLAR: Yes, it's very depressing.

YOUNG LADY: There, you see! And what if that's to be my fate? I'm expected to get married. Do you know for sure that not everyone is a scoundrel?

SCHOLAR: I know it for a fact. After all, I'm an historian.

YOUNG LADY: That would be nice! However, I don't believe you.

SCHOLAR: Why not?

YOUNG LADY: On principle I don't believe anyone or anything.

SCHOLAR: That can't be. You have such a healthful complexion, such sparkling eyes. If you don't believe in anything, that's deadly!

YOUNG LADY: Ah, I understand everything.

SCHOLAR: To understand everything is deadly too.

YOUNG LADY: Everything in the world is the same. That lot's right and this lot's right, and, at the end of the day, I couldn't care less.

SCHOLAR: You couldn't care less—that's worse than deadly! You can't think like that. No! How you grieve me!

YOUNG LADY: I don't care... No, I don't care about anything, it seems. So now you won't have to stare at me every evening any more.

SCHOLAR: I will. Things are not as simple as they seem. I believed that your thoughts were as harmonious as you are... But when they're revealed to me... They don't at all resemble the ones I expected... And even so...even so I love you...

YOUNG LADY: You love me?

SCHOLAR: I love you...

YOUNG LADY: Look at that...I understood everything, believed in nothing at all, nothing mattered to me, and now it's all upside-down...

SCHOLAR: I love you...

YOUNG LADY: Go away... Or don't... No, go away and shut the door... No, I'll go away... But...if you dare tomorrow evening...dare not to come out on the balcony, I...I...shall order...no...I shall simply be disappointed. *(Goes to the door, turns around)* I don't even know your name.

SCHOLAR: My name is Christian Theodor.

YOUNG LADY: Good-bye, Christian Theodor, my dear.
Please don't smile! Don't assume that you've cleverly
tricked me. No, don't be distressed…I'm just talking…
When you told me suddenly, straight out, that you
love me, I got flushed, even though I've come out
on the balcony in a flimsy dress. Don't you dare talk
to me! That'll do! If I hear another word, I shall start
to cry. Good-bye! …What an unhappy girl I am, sir.
(Exits)

SCHOLAR: That's that…I thought that one more
second—and I would understand everything, but
now I think that one more second—and I'll be totally
confused. I'm afraid that this young lady is actually
the princess. "Everyone is a scoundrel, everything on
earth is the same, nothing matters to me, and I don't
believe in anything." —what clear signs of pernicious
anemia, common to delicate persons who've grown
up in a hothouse atmosphere! …Her… she… But even
so she suddenly got flushed, when I confessed that I
love her! Does that mean she's got enough blood in her
veins? *(Laughs.)* I'm sure, I'm sure that it will all have
a happy ending. Shadow, my kind, obedient shadow!
You lie so humbly at my feet. Your head glances at
the door through which my unknown young lady left.
You ought to get up, shadow, and go over to her. What
does it cost you! You should up and say to her: "This
is all nonsense. My master loves you, loves you so all
will be well. If you are a frog princess, he will bring
you back to life and turn you into a beautiful woman."
In short, you know what you have to say, after all we
grew up together. *(Laughs.)* Go!

*(The SCHOLAR walks away from the door. His SHADOW
suddenly separates from him. It draws itself up to its full
height on the balcony across the way. It plunges through the
door which the young lady, on her way out, left half open.*

SCHOLAR: What's this…I have a funny feeling in my legs… throughout my whole body… Am I…am I falling ill? I… *(Staggers, falls into an armchair, rings)*

(ANNUNCIATA runs in.)

SCHOLAR: Annunciata! It turns out you were right.

ANNUNCIATA: It was the princess?

SCHOLAR: No! I've fallen ill. *(Closes his eyes)*

ANNUNCIATA: *(Runs to the door.)* Father!

(PIETRO enters.)

PIETRO: Don't holler! Don't you know your father is right there eavesdroppin' at the door.

ANNUNCIATA: I didn't notice.

PIETRO: Doesn't notice her own father… What's the world comin' to! Well? What're you blinkin' for? Figger on bawlin' again?

ANNUNCIATA: He's fallen ill.

PIETRO: Let me, sir, help put you to bed.

SCHOLAR: *(Gets up)* No. I can do it myself. Please don't touch me…

PIETRO: What're you afraid of? I won't eat you!

SCHOLAR: I'm not so sure. I've suddenly got weak. *(Goes to the screen that conceals his bed)*

ANNUNCIATA: *(Quietly, in terror.)* Look!

PIETRO: What now?

ANNUNCIATA: He's got no shadow.

PIETRO: That so? He really don't… Damn climate! And how did he manage that? There'll be rumors. People'll think it's an epidemic.

(The SCHOLAR goes behind the screen.)

PIETRO: Not a word to nobody. You hear?

ANNUNCIATA: *(By the screen)* He's fainted.

PIETRO: Better and better. Run for the doctor. The doctor'll confine him to bed for a week or two, and in the meantime he'll grow a new shadow. And nobody'll be the wiser.

ANNUNCIATA: The man without a shadow -- that's one of the most distressing fairy tales in the world.

PIETRO: I'm tellin' you he'll grow a new shadow! He'll get outa this mess… Scram!

(ANNUNCIATA runs out.)

PIETRO: What the hell… It's a lucky thing that newspaper feller's busy with the lady and ain't got wind o' this.

(CESARE BORGIA enters.)

CESARE BORGIA: Good evening!

PIETRO: Ah, speak o' the devil… Damn… Where's your bit o' fluff?

CESARE BORGIA: She went to the concert.

PIETRO: All concerts can go to hell!

CESARE BORGIA: The scholar has fainted?

PIETRO: Yes, blast him.

CESARE BORGIA: Did you hear?

PIETRO: What exactly?

CESARE BORGIA: His conversation with the princess.

PIETRO: Yes.

CESARE BORGIA: A short answer. How come you're not cussing out everyone and everything, or shooting your pistol, or shouting?

PIETRO: When things is serious I'm calm.

CESARE BORGIA: Like when it turns out to be the real princess.

PIETRO: Yes. It's her.

CESARE BORGIA: I can see you'd like him to marry the princess.

PIETRO: Me? I'd devour him the first chance I got.

CESARE BORGIA: He's got to be devoured. Yes, got to, got to. In my opinion, this is the most opportune moment. It's easiest of all to devour a man when he's sick or gone on vacation. Then he hasn't a clue who's devouring him and you can stay on the best of terms with him.

PIETRO: The shadow.

CESARE BORGIA: What shadow?

PIETRO: We gotta find his shadow.

CESARE BORGIA: What for?

PIETRO: It'll help us. It'll never forgive him in this lifetime that once it was his shadow.

CESARE BORGIA: Yes, it will help us devour him.

PIETRO: The shadow is the complete opposite of the Scholar.

CESARE BORGIA: But…then it might prove to be stronger than we suppose.

PIETRO: So what? The shadow won't forget that we helped it enter society. And we shall devour him.

CESARE BORGIA: Yes, we've got to devour him. We've got to, got to!

PIETRO: Hush!

(ANNUNCIATA *runs in.*)

ANNUNCIATA: Get out of here! What are you doing there?

PIETRO: Daughter! *(Gets the pistol.)* Anyhow, come to my place. We'll talk it over there. Is the doctor on his way?

ANNUNCIATA: Yes, he's running as fast as his legs can carry him. He says it's a serious case.

PIETRO: All right.

(CESARE BORGIA *and* PIETRO *exit.)*

ANNUNCIATA: *(Glancing behind the screen)* I knew it! His face is as peaceful and kindly as if he were dreaming about a walk in the woods beneath the trees. No, they'll never forgive him for being such a good man! Something's going to happen, something's going to happen!

(Curtain)

END OF ACT ONE

ACT TWO

(A park. A little square strewn with sand, hedged round by topiary. In the distance a gazebo. The MAJOR-DOMO *and his* AIDE *are fussing about the forestage.)*

MAJOR-DOMO: Put the table here. And the armchairs here. Put the chess-board and pieces on the table. That's it. Now everything's set for the meeting.

AIDE: But tell me, Major-Domo sir, why are the honorable cabinet ministers meeting here in a park, and not in the palace?

MAJOR-DOMO: Because there are walls in the palace. Get me?

AIDE: Not quite.

MAJOR-DOMO: And walls have ears. Get me?

AIDE: Yes, now I've got you.

MAJOR-DOMO: Precisely. Put cushions on this chair.

AIDE: Is that for the honorable Prime Minister?

MAJOR-DOMO: No. It's for the honorable Finance Minister. He is gravely ill.

AIDE: What's wrong with him?

MAJOR-DOMO: He is the richest businessman in the land. His competitors hate him to death. And last year one of them stooped to crime. He decided to poison the honorable Finance Minister.

AIDE: How horrible!

MAJOR-DOMO: Don't be appalled before the time comes. The honorable Finance Minister found out about it in time and bought up all the poisons in the land.

AIDE: How fortunate!

MAJOR-DOMO: Don't rejoice before the time comes. Then the guilty party went to the honorable Finance Minister and offered him an unusually high price for the poisons. And the honorable Finance Minister acted in a totally natural way. After all, the Minister is a pragmatic politician. He figured out the profit angle and sold the scoundrel his whole supply of toxins. And the scoundrel poisoned the Minister. His Excellency's whole family was pleased to die in excruciating torments. And ever since he's barely hanging on to life, but he cleared a two hundred percent profit on the deal. Business is business. Get me?

AIDE: Yes, now I got you.

MAJOR-DOMO: Well, precisely. So, is everything ready? The chairs. The chess set. Today's an especially important conference.

AIDE: Why do you think so?

MAJOR-DOMO: In the first place, the two most important cabinet ministers—the Prime and the Finance—are meeting, and in the second, they will pretend to be playing chess, and not conferring. Everyone knows what that means. The shrubbery is probably swarming with busybodies.

AIDE: But suppose the busybodies overhear what the honorable ministers say?

MAJOR-DOMO: The busybodies will be none the wiser.

AIDE: Why not?

MAJOR-DOMO: Because the honorable ministers communicate in half-words. You can learn a lot from half-words! *(Suddenly bows low.)* They're coming. I've served at court so long that my waist bends by itself whenever high dignitaries approach. I may not hear or see them yet, but I'm already bowing. That's why I'm in charge. Get me? Bow down! ...Lower.

(The MAJOR-DOMO *stoops to the ground. The Aide imitates him. From either side of the stage, right and left, the two ministers enter simultaneously—the* FINANCE MINISTER *and the* PRIME MINISTER. *The latter is short, paunchy, balding, ruddy, a bit over fifty. The* FINANCE MINISTER *is wizened, lanky, looking round in alarm, limping on both legs. He is borne under his arms by two strapping* LACKEYS. *The* FINANCE MINISTER *and the* PRIME MINISTER *simultaneously walk up to the table, simultaneously sit down and immediately set about playing chess. The* LACKEYS *who carry the* FINANCE MINISTER, *once they've seated him, silently withdraw. The* MAJOR-DOMO *and his* AIDE *remain on stage. They stand at attention.)*

PRIME MINISTER: Health?

FINANCE MINISTER: Abys.

PRIME MINISTER: Business?

FINANCE MINISTER: Rot.

PRIME MINISTER: Why?

FINANCE MINISTER: Compet.

(The FINANCE MINISTER *and the* PRIME MINISTER *play chess in silence.)*

MAJOR-DOMO: *(Whispers.)* You see, I told you they communicate in half words.

PRIME MINISTER: Heard about the princess?

FINANCE MINISTER: Had a rep.

PRIME MINISTER: This travelling scholar has stolen her heart.

FINANCE MINISTER: Stolen?! Wait... Lackeys! No, not you... My lackeys!

(One of the LACKEYS *who carried in the* FINANCE MINISTER *enters.*

FINANCE MINISTER: Lackey! Did you lock all the doors when we left?

LACKEY: Yes, your excellency.

FINANCE MINISTER: The iron one?

LACKEY: Quite so.

FINANCE MINISTER: And the copper one?

LACKEY: Quite so.

FINANCE MINISTER: And the cast-iron one?

LACKEY: Quite so.

FINANCE MINISTER: And you set up the man-traps? Remember, you will answer with your life for the least loss.

LACKEY: I remember, your excellency.

FINANCE MINISTER: You may go...

(The LACKEY *exits.)*

FINANCE MINISTER: I'm listening.

PRIME MINISTER: According to the reports of the Privy Councilors on duty, the day before yesterday the princess looked in the mirror for a long time, then burst into tears and said *(Pulls out a notebook, reads)* "Ah, why am I wasting away to no avail?" and for the fifth time sent to ask after the Scholar's health. When she learned that no special changes had occurred, the princess stamped her foot and exclaimed *(Reads)*

"Damn it to hell!" And today she named a rendezvous with him here in the park. There. How do you li?

FINANCE MINISTER: Definitely don't li! Who's this scholar?

PRIME MINISTER: Ah, I've made the most minute study of him.

FINANCE MINISTER: A blackmailer?

PRIME MINISTER: Worse...

FINANCE MINISTER: A thief?

PRIME MINISTER: Even worse.

FINANCE MINISTER: A conman, a wise guy, a slippery character?

PRIME MINISTER: If only...

FINANCE MINISTER: Then what is he at last?

PRIME MINISTER: A simple, naïve human being.

FINANCE MINISTER: Check to your king.

PRIME MINISTER: I castle...

FINANCE MINISTER: Check to your queen.

PRIME MINISTER: Poor princess! We could expose a blackmailer, catch a thief, outsmart a slippery character and a wise guy, but this... The actions of simple, honest people are sometimes so puzzling!

FINANCE MINISTER: Have to either bri him or murd.

PRIME MINISTER: Yes, there's no other solution.

FINANCE MINISTER: Has the town got wi of all this?

PRIME MINISTER: How could it not get wi?

FINANCE MINISTER: I knew it. That's why prudent people are sending their gold abroad in such quantities. Day before yesterday a certain banker even sent abroad his gold teeth. And now he keeps going back and forth across the border. In his native land he's now got no way to chew his food.

PRIME MINISTER: In my opinion, your banker displayed needless anxiety.

FINANCE MINISTER: It's keen intuition! There's no more sensitive organism on earth than financial circles. A single royal proclamation caused seven bankruptcies, seven suicides, and a seven point drop in the stock market. And now... Oh, what's going to happen now! No changes, honorable Prime Minister! Life must go on regularly, like clockwork.

PRIME MINISTER: By the way, what time is it?

FINANCE MINISTER: My gold watch has been sent abroad. And if I carry the silver one, there'll be rumors that I'm ruined and there'll be a panic in financial circles.

PRIME MINISTER: Isn't there any gold left in our country?

FINANCE MINISTER: More than we need.

PRIME MINISTER: Where from?

FINANCE MINISTER: From across the border. Transnational financial circles are agitated for their own reasons and are transferring gold to us. So we're all right. Let's finish this. In conclusion, we shall buy off the scholar.

PRIME MINISTER: Or kill him off.

FINANCE MINISTER: How should we do it?

PRIME MINISTER: The most delicate way! After all, a feeling such as love is involved in this matter! I intend to soften up the scholar with the aid of friendship.

FINANCE MINISTER: Friendship?

PRIME MINISTER: Yes. For this we need to find a man who's friendly with the scholar. A friend will know what he likes, how he might be bought. A friend will know what he hates, what will spell sheer death to him. I shall order the head office to procure a friend.

FINANCE MINISTER: That's a terrible idea.

PRIME MINISTER: Why?

FINANCE MINISTER: After all, the scholar is on his travels, which means we'd have to order a friend from abroad! And in which column am I to enter that expense? Any havoc in the cost estimate makes my chief bookkeeper shed bitter tears. He will sob like a child, and then will fall into a delirium. In no time at all he'll stop paying out money in general. To everybody. Even me. Even you.

PRIME MINISTER: Is that so? That's unpleasant. So the fate of the whole kingdom rests on a single card. What next?

FINANCE MINISTER: I don't know.

PRIME MINISTER: But who does know?

AIDE: *(Stepping forward)* I do.

FINANCE MINISTER: *(leaping up.)* What's this? Is it starting?

PRIME MINISTER: Calm down, please. If it were to start anywhere, it won't be with palace lackeys.

FINANCE MINISTER: So there isn't a rebellion?

PRIME MINISTER: No. It's mere insolence. Who are you?

AIDE: I'm the man you're looking for. I am a friend of the scholar, his closest friend. We haven't been separated from the cradle to these last few days.

PRIME MINISTER: Listen, my good man, do you know with whom you're speaking?

AIDE: Yes.

PRIME MINISTER: Then why don't you call me "your excellency"?

AIDE: *(With a deep bow)* Forgive me, your excellency.

PRIME MINISTER: You've just arrived here?

AIDE: I came into the world in this town, your excellency.

PRIME MINISTER: And nevertheless you're a friend of this newly-arrived scholar?

AIDE: I am precisely the man you need, your excellency. I know him like nobody else, and he doesn't know me at all, your excellency.

PRIME MINISTER: Strange.

AIDE: If you like, I shall tell you who I am, your excellency.

PRIME MINISTER: Tell me. Why are you looking around?

AIDE: Let me write who I am in the sand, your excellency.

PRIME MINISTER: Do so.

(The AIDE draws something in the sand. The FINANCE MINISTER and the PRIME MINISTER read it and look at one another.)

PRIME MINISTER: What do you th?

FINANCE MINISTER: Might wor. But be caref! Or he'll ask an exorbitant pri.

PRIME MINISTER: All right. Who arranged for you to work in the palace?

AIDE: The Honorable Cesare Borgia and the Honorable Pietro, your excellency.

PRIME MINISTER: *(To the* FINANCE MINISTER.*)* You know those names?

FINANCE MINISTER: Yes, wholly trustworthy ogres.

PRIME MINISTER: Very well, my good sir, we shall think it over.

AIDE: Dare I remind you that we are in the south, your excellency.

PRIME MINISTER: So what?

AIDE: In the south everything grows rapidly, your excellency. The scholar and the princess began talking only two weeks ago and haven't met once since then, but look how their love has grown, your excellency. What if we're too late, your excellency!

PRIME MINISTER: I told you we will think it over. Stand to one side.

(The FINANCE MINISTER *and the* PRIME MINISTER *confer.)*

PRIME MINISTER: Come over here, my good man.

(The AIDE *obeys.)*

PRIME MINISTER: We have thought it over and decided to appoint you to the Prime Ministerial Head Office.

AIDE: Thank you, your excellency. In my opinion, here's how you should deal with the scholar...

PRIME MINISTER: What's wrong with you, my good man? Are you planning to act before you've executed any of the formalities? Have you gone crazy? Don't you know what a government office is all about?

AIDE: Forgive me, your excellency.

(A burst of loud laughter offstage.)

PRIME MINISTER: Here come the spa-goers. They will get in our way. Let's go to the head office and there we shall formalize your appointment. After that, all right, we'll listen to you.

AIDE: Thank you, your excellency.

FINANCE MINISTER: Lackeys!

(The LACKEYS *appear.)*

FINANCE MINISTER: Take me away from here.

(They exit. The doors to the gazebo are flung open, and the DOCTOR *appears from within—a young man, exceptionally gloomy and preoccupied. The* SPA-GOERS, *in lightweight but luxurious clothing, surround him.)*

1ST FEMALE SPA-GOER: Doctor, why do I have a feeling under my knee that's like thinking?

DOCTOR: Which knee?

1ST FEMALE SPA-GOER: The right one.

DOCTOR: It'll pass.

2ND FEMALE SPA-GOER: And why at meals, between the eighth and ninth course, do I have melancholy thoughts?

DOCTOR: What kind, for instance?

2ND FEMALE SPA-GOER: Well, I suddenly want to go far away into a desert and there dedicate myself to prayers and fasting.

DOCTOR: It'll pass.

1ST MALE SPA-GOER: Doctor, why after the fortieth bath have I suddenly stopped liking brunettes?

DOCTOR: And whom do you like now?

1ST MALE SPA-GOER: One particular little blonde.

DOCTOR: It'll pass. My friends, may I remind you that the consultation hour is over. Sister of mercy, you are off-duty. Sister of mirth, resume your duties.

SISTER OF MIRTH: Who wants to play ball? Who's for skipping-rope? Hoops, hoops, ladies and gentlemen! Who want to play tag? I spy? Cat-and-mouse? Time's

on the wing, ladies and gentlemen, whoop it up, ladies
and gentlemen, play games!

(The SPA-GOERS *disperse, playing games. The* SCHOLAR
and ANNUNCIATA *enter.)*

ANNUNCIATA: Doctor, he just bought a whole tray of
fruit lozenges.

SCHOLAR: But I distribute the lozenges among the
ragamuffins in the street.

ANNUNCIATA: Doesn't matter! Should a sick man be
buying sweets?

DOCTOR: *(To the* SCHOLAR*)* Stand facing the sun. So.
Your shadow has grown to normal proportions. That
was to be expected -- in the south everything grows so
quickly. How do you feel?

SCHOLAR: I feel completely healthy.

DOCTOR: All the same I'll sound you out. No need to
take off your coat: I have very sensitive hearing. *(Takes
a stethoscope from a table in the gazebo)* Now. Heave a
sigh. Heave a deep sigh. Sigh heavily. Once more. Sigh
with relief. Once more. Look at the world through your
fingers. Wave everything away with your hand. Once
more. Shrug your shoulders. So. *(Sits down and falls into
thought)*

ANNUNCIATA: Well, what do you say, doctor? How is
his case?

DOCTOR: Bad.

ANNUNCIATA: There, you see, and he says he's
completely healthy.

DOCTOR: Yes, he's healthy. But his case is in a bad
way. And it will get even worse, until he learns how
to look at the world through his fingers, how to wave
everything away with his hand, how to master the art
of shrugging his shoulders.

ANNUNCIATA: How can he, doctor? How can he learn all that?

(*The* DOCTOR *silently shrugs his shoulders.*)

ANNUNCIATA: Answer me, doctor. Please. Otherwise I won't leave you in peace, you know how stubborn I am. What does he have to do?

DOCTOR: Take care!

ANNUNCIATA: But he's smiling.

DOCTOR: Yes, that happens.

ANNUNCIATA: He's a scholar, he's clever, he's older than me, but sometimes I simply want to spank him. Well, say something to him.

(*The* DOCTOR *waves his hand in dismissal.*)

ANNUNCIATA: Doctor!

DOCTOR: You can see he won't listen to me. He's got his nose buried in some papers.

ANNUNCIATA: It's a letter from the Princess. Sir! The Doctor wants to talk to you but you're not listening.

SCHOLAR: What do you mean? I'm always listening.

ANNUNCIATA: And what do you say to this?

SCHOLAR: I say, I say...

ANNUNCIATA: Sir!

SCHOLAR: Right away! I can't find the passage... (*Mutters*) How did she put it—"ever yours" or "forever yours"?

ANNUNCIATA: (*Plaintively.*) I'll shoot you!

SCHOLAR: Yes, yes, please do.

DOCTOR: Christian-Theodor! You are a scholar, aren't you... Pay heed to me once and for all. After all, I'm a colleague of yours.

SCHOLAR: *(Putting the letter away)* Yes, yes. Forgive me.

DOCTOR: In folk tales about the man who lost his shadow, in the monographs of Chamisso and your friend Hans Christian Andersen it is said that...

SCHOLAR: Let's not refer to what's been said. With me there'll be a different ending.

DOCTOR: Answer me as a doctor—do you plan to marry the Princess?

SCHOLAR: Of course.

DOCTOR: But I heard that you dream of making people as happy as possible.

SCHOLAR: And that's true.

DOCTOR: They can't both be true.

SCHOLAR: Why not?

DOCTOR: Once you've married the Princess, you'll become king.

SCHOLAR: That's what's so great about it—I won't be king! The Princess loves me, and she'll go away with me. And we'll relinquish the crown—you see, how good that is! And I will explain to anyone who asks and din it into the head of even the least inquisitive: royal power is idiotic and insignificant. And that's why I abdicated the throne.

DOCTOR: And people will understand you?

SCHOLAR: Of course! After all, I'm living proof of it.

(The DOCTOR silently waves his hand in dismissal.)

SCHOLAR: You can explain anything to a person. After all, he understands the alphabet and this is even simpler than the alphabet, and, more important, is more relevant to himself!

(The SPA-GOERS cross the stage, playing games.)

DOCTOR: *(Indicating them.)* And they too will understand you?

SCHOLAR: Of course! There's something alive in every human being. All you have to do is touch his vital spot.

DOCTOR: You're a child! I know them better. They come to me to be cured.

SCHOLAR: What's wrong with them?

DOCTOR: An acute form of satiety.

SCHOLAR: Is it dangerous?

DOCTOR: Yes, for those around them.

SCHOLAR: How so?

DOCTOR: An acute form of satiety can suddenly take possession of even decent people. A man has earned a lot of money in an honest way. And suddenly he exhibits a morbid symptom: the specific, restless, hungry look of the well-to-do. That's the end of him. From that point on he's sterile, blind and cruel.

SCHOLAR: But didn't you try to explain it all to him?

DOCTOR: That's why I wanted to put you on your guard against this. Woe betide the man who tries to make them think about anything except money. It drives them into actual madness.

(The SPA-GOERS *run through.)*

SCHOLAR: Look, they're having such a good time!

DOCTOR: They're on vacation!

*(*GIULIA *quickly enters.)*

GIULIA: *(To the* DOCTOR.*)* There you are at last. Are you quite well?

DOCTOR: Yes, Giulia.

GIULIA: Ah, it's the doctor.

DOCTOR: Yes, it is I, Giulia.

GIULIA: Why are you looking at me like a lovelorn rabbit? Beat it!

(The DOCTOR *wants to reply, but goes into the gazebo, silently waving his hand in dismissal.)*

GIULIA: Where are you, Christian-Theodor?

SCHOLAR: Here I am.

GIULIA: *(Walks up to him)* Yes, that's you. *(Smiles)* How glad I am to see you! Well, what was that nonentity of a doctor telling you?

SCHOLAR: He was telling me I'm healthy. Why do you call him a nonentity?

GIULIA: Ah, I loved him once, but then I hate such people awfully.

SCHOLAR: It was unrequited love?

GIULIA: Worse. That very doctor has an ugly, malicious wife who scares him to death. You can only kiss him on the nape of his neck.

SCHOLAR: Why?

GIULIA: He's always turning around to see if his wife is coming. But that's enough about him. I came here to… warn you, Christian-Theodor. Trouble lies in wait for you.

SCHOLAR: Impossible. I'm so happy!

GIULIA: Nevertheless trouble lies in wait for you.

ANNUNCIATA: Please stop smiling, madam, I beseech you. Otherwise we won't know whether you're serious or joking, and we may even perish for that reason.

GIULIA: Never mind my smiling. In our club, the club of real people, everyone smiles no matter what. That way, anything you say can be interpreted every which way. I'm speaking seriously, Christian-Theodor. Trouble lies in wait for you.

SCHOLAR: What kind?

GIULIA: I told you that a member of our club is a cabinet minister?

SCHOLAR: Yes.

GIULIA: He's the Finance Minister. He joined our club on account of me. He's wooing me and is constantly on the verge of proposing to me.

ANNUNCIATA: Him? He can't even walk!

GIULIA: Lackeys in spiffy uniforms move him around. He is so rich. And I ran into him just now. And he asked where I was going. When he heard your name, he scowled, Christian-Theodor.

ANNUNCIATA: How awful!

GIULIA: In our club we all share a particular skill—we have an amazing ability to read the faces of officials. And even I, for all my being nearsighted, just now read on the minister's face that someone is brewing something against you, Christian-Theodor.

SCHOLAR: Well, let it brew.

GIULIA: Ah, you've ruined me in these last two weeks. Why did I ever get to know you? I've turned into a sentimental housewife. What a nuisance! Annunciata, take him away from here.

SCHOLAR: Why?

GIULIA: The Finance Minister will be here any minute, so I'll put all my charms in play and find out what they're cooking up. I'll even try to save you, Christian-Theodor.

ANNUNCIATA: How can I thank you, madam?

GIULIA: Not a word to anyone, if you really want to thank me. Go away.

ANNUNCIATA: Let's go, sir.

SCHOLAR: Annunciata, you know very well that I have to be here to meet the princess.

GIULIA: You've still got an hour. Go away, if you love the princess and feel anything for me.

SCHOLAR: Good-bye, poor Giulia. How you both worry! And I'm the only one who knows—things will have a happy ending.

ANNUNCIATA: He's coming. Sir, I beg you...

GIULIA: Hush! I told you, I'll try.

(The SCHOLAR *and* ANNUNCIATA *exit. The* FINANCE MINISTER *appears, borne by his* LACKEYS.*)*

FINANCE MINISTER: Lackeys! Seat me next to that fascinating woman. Put me in a pose suitable for light, witty conservation.

(The LACKEYS *step forward.)*

FINANCE MINISTER: All right, you may go now.

(The LACKEYS *exit.)*

FINANCE MINISTER: Giulia, I want to make you happy.

GIULIA: That's easy enough for you to do.

FINANCE MINISTER: Fascinating woman! Circe! Aphrodite! We were just talking about you in the Prime Minister's Head Office.

GIULIA: Naughty boys!

FINANCE MINISTER: I assure you! And we all agreed that you are a clever, practical nymph!

GIULIA: The things courtiers say!

FINANCE MINISTER: And we decided that you are just the one to help us in a certain matter.

GIULIA: Tell me which one. If it's not too hard, I'm ready to help you in anything.

FINANCE MINISTER: A trifle! You have to help us annihilate the travelling scholar, Theodor-Christian by name. You are acquainted with him, aren't you? You'll help us?

(GIULIA *does not answer.*)

FINANCE MINISTER: Lackeys!

(*The* LACKEYS *appear.*)

FINANCE MINISTER: The pose of extreme surprise!

(*The* LACKEYS *obey.*)

FINANCE MINISTER: Giulia, I am extremely surprised. Why do you look at me as if you didn't know how to answer?

GIULIA: As a matter of fact I don't know what to tell you. These last two weeks have simply ruined me.

FINANCE MINISTER: I don't understand.

GIULIA: I don't understand myself.

FINANCE MINISTER: You refuse?

GIULIA: I don't know.

FINANCE MINISTER: Lackeys!

(*The* LACKEYS *run in.*)

FINANCE MINISTER: The pose of extreme indignation.

(*The* LACKEYS *obey.*)

FINANCE MINISTER: I am extremely indignant, Miss Giulia Giuli! What is the meaning of this? You haven't fallen in love with this beggarly brat, have you? Silence! On your feet! Hands at your sides! Before you is not a man, but a Finance Minister. Your refusal shows that you do not sufficiently respect our whole System of Government. Hold your tongue! Silence! Arrest her!

GIULIA: Wait a minute!

FINANCE MINISTER: I will not wait a minute! "Why Am
I Not a Forest Glade!" Only now I understand what
you mean by that. You're hinting that the farmers
have too little land. Eh? What? I'm going to…I shall…
Tomorrow the newspapers will tear to shreds your
face, your singing style, your private life. Lackeys! Foot
stamp!

(The LACKEYS *stamp their feet.)*

FINANCE MINISTER: Not your feet, blockheads, mine!

(The LACKEYS *obey.)*

FINANCE MINISTER: Good day to you, ex-celebrity!

GIULIA: Wait a minute!

FINANCE MINISTER: I will not!

GIULIA: Look at me!

FINANCE MINISTER: Take the trouble to call me "Your
Excellency"!

GIULIA: Look at me, Your Excellency.

FINANCE MINISTER: Well?

GIULIA: Can't you understand that for me there has
always been no greater man than the Minister of
Finance?

FINANCE MINISTER: *(Flattered)* Now, cut that out!

GIULIA: I give you my word. And how can one say
"yes" to such a man right away?

FINANCE MINISTER: Aphrodite! In other words, you
agree?

GIULIA: Now my answer is—yes.

FINANCE MINISTER: Lackeys, embrace!

(The LACKEYS *embrace* GIULIA.*)*

FINANCE MINISTER: Blockheads! I want to embrace her.
That's it. Dearest Giulia, thank you. Tomorrow by a

decree from the Head Office I shall announce myself
your biggest fan. Lackeys! Seat me beside this goddess
of love. Put me in the pose of extreme lightheartedness.
And you, Giulia, take a lighthearted pose, but listen
to me with both ears. Now then, in a short while you
will find the Scholar engaged in a lively conversation
with the Official for Top Priority Cases. And on some
pretext you will take the Scholar away from here for
about twenty minutes. That's all there is to it.

GIULIA: That's all?

FINANCE MINISTER: You see how simple it is! And just
those twenty minutes will spell his doom once and
for all. Let's go to the jeweller's, I'll buy you a ring of
incalculable value. Let's be on our way. Lackeys! Carry
us off.

(They withdraw. Enter the AIDE, *then* PIETRO *and* CESARE
BORGIA.*)*

AIDE: Good afternoon, gentlemen!

PIETRO: Well, we already met this morning, didn't we?

AIDE: I advise you to forget that we met this morning.
I won't forget that once upon a time you found me, set
me up in the palace, helped me to enter society. But
you, gentlemen, must forget once and for all who I was
and remember who I became.

CESARE BORGIA: Just who are you now?

AIDE: Now I am the Official for Top Priority Cases in
the Head Office of His Excellency the Prime Minister.

CESARE BORGIA: How did you manage that? What a
success story! Who the hell knows what it is! That's
how it goes!

AIDE: I achieved this success by my own abilities.
Therefore I remind you twice over: forget who I was.

PIETRO: Forgetting's possible. If we don't fall out, what's there to remember?

CESARE BORGIA: It isn't easy to forget about this. But it's possible to keep silent from time to time. You catch my drift?

AIDE: I do, gentlemen. We won't fall out, so long as you keep silent about who I was. Now pay close attention. I've been assigned Case number 8989. *(Displays the file folder)* Here it is.

PIETRO: *(Reads.)* Case of the Princess's Marriage.

AIDE: Yes. Here in this file is the whole affair: the princess and him and you, present and future.

CESARE BORGIA: Who's the intended fiancé of this lofty personage doesn't much concern me, like everything else in this, as the saying goes, earthly life, and yet...

AIDE: You're both intended fiancés of the princess.

PIETRO: What the hell! How the both of us?

CESARE BORGIA: He and I?

AIDE: Yes. After all, the princess has to have an assortment to choose from.

CESARE BORGIA: But you should see to this yourself!

PIETRO: What the devil does she need him for, if I'm the one!

AIDE: Quiet! It has been decided. I propose the princess make a choice. Pietro, take your daughter home. I have to talk to the scholar, and she protects him like a whole regiment of guards.

CESARE BORGIA: She's in love with him. But Pietro is blind as a father should be!

PIETRO: Damnation! I'll kill 'em both!

CESARE BORGIA: About time too.

PIETRO: You Satan! You're egging me on on purpose! They'll arrest me for murder, and you'll be the only fiancé? Is that what you want?

CESARE BORGIA: Yes, I do. And it's a perfectly natural wish. Good-bye.

PIETRO: Oh no, you're going nowhere. I know where you're headed.

CESARE BORGIA: Where?

PIETRO: You want to devour me one way or another. Don't you move. I won't stir a step from you.

AIDE: Hush. He's on his way here. Let's settle it this way: the one who becomes king will make the other a big compensation. He'll appoint the loser First Royal Secretary, for instance, or Captain of the Guard. Look out: here he comes. He looks cheerful.

CESARE BORGIA: But what will you talk to him about?

AIDE: I talk to everyone in his own language.

(Enter the SCHOLAR *and* ANNUNCIATA.*)*

SCHOLAR: What a beautiful day, gentlemen!

PIETRO: Yes, nothin' wrong with the day, damn and blast it. Annunciata, home!

ANNUNCIATA: Papa…

PIETRO: Home! Otherwise it'll be the worse for you and somebody else. You didn't even tell the cook what to make for dinner today.

ANNUNCIATA: I don't care.

PIETRO: What are you saying, you freak! Mister Cesare Borgia, let's go home together, friend, or, on my honor, I'll neatly polish you off with a dagger.

(They exit. The AIDE, *having stood aside during the preceding dialogue, walks up to the* SCHOLAR.*)*

AIDE: Do you recognize me?

SCHOLAR: Forgive me, no.

AIDE: Take a closer look.

SCHOLAR: What's this? I feel I know you, and know you well, but...

AIDE: We've lived together for so many years.

SCHOLAR: What are you saying?

AIDE: I assure you. I dogged your footsteps faithfully, but you only rarely cast a careless glance at me. In fact I was often above you, rising to the roof of the tallest houses. This usually occurred on moonlit nights.

SCHOLAR: Then, that means, you...

AIDE: Hush! Yes, I am your shadow... Why do you look at me so incredulously? After all I've been bound to you all your life from the day you were born.

SCHOLAR: But no, I simply...

SHADOW: You're angry with me for abandoning you. But you yourself asked me to go to the princess, and I hastened to carry out your request. After all, we grew up together among the very same people. When you said "mama", I soundlessly repeated those words. I loved those whom you loved, and your enemies were my enemies. When you fell ill, I couldn't even lift my head from the pillow. You put on weight and so did I. Can it be that after a whole lifetime lived in such close friendship I could suddenly become your enemy!

SCHOLAR: But no, how can you! Do sit down, old friend. I was sick without you, but now everything's right again...I feel good. Today is such a beautiful day. I'm happy, my soul is free today—here am I telling you, although as you know, I don't like this kind of talk. But you simply touched me... But, what about

you, what have you doing all this time, my good sir? ...
Or no, wait, let's begin on a first name basis.

(SHADOW, *shaking the* SCHOLAR's *hand:*)

SHADOW: Thank you. I remained your shadow, that's
what I've been doing all this time.

SCHOLAR: I don't understand.

SHADOW: You sent me to the princess. At first I set
myself up as aide to the Head Lackey in the palace,
then rose higher and higher, and from today on I'm the
Prime Minister's Official for Top Priority Cases.

SCHOLAR: Poor fellow! I can imagine how hard it is to
be among those people! But why did you do it?

SHADOW: For your sake.

SCHOLAR: My sake?

SHADOW: You have no idea what savage hatred
surrounds you ever since you fell in love with the
princess and she with you. They're all ready to devour
you, and would have devoured you today, if it weren't
for me.

SCHOLAR: What're you on about!

SHADOW: I go amongst them in order to protect you.
They trust me. They assigned me Case no. 8989.

SCHOLAR: What's that?

SHADOW: It's the case of the princess's marriage.

SCHOLAR: It can't be.

SHADOW: And luckily for us this case fell into the right
hands. The Prime Minister himself sent me to you. My
orders are to buy you off.

SCHOLAR: Buy me off? (*Laughs*) For how much?

SHADOW: Peanuts. They promise you fame, honor and
wealth, if you turn down the princess.

SCHOLAR: And if I don't sell myself?

SHADOW: They'll kill you this very day.

SCHOLAR: Never in my life could I believe I can die, especially today.

SHADOW: Christian, my friend, my brother, they will kill you, believe me. Do they know the paths we ran along in childhood, to the mill where we chatted with the water-sprite, the forest where we met the schoolmaster's daughter and fell in love—you with her, and I with her shadow. They cannot even imagine that you are a living human being. For them you are an impediment like a tree stump or a roadblock. Believe me, before the sun sets, you will be a dead man.

SCHOLAR: What do you advise me to do?

SHADOW: *(Pulls a piece of paper out of the file folder)* Sign this.

SCHOLAR: *(Reads.)* "I, the undersigned, resolutely, irrevocably and conclusively refuse to enter into marriage with the princess, heiress apparent to the kingdom, if in recompense for this I am guaranteed fame, honor and riches." You seriously expect me to sign this?

SHADOW: Sign if you're not a child, if you're a real human being.

SCHOLAR: What's come over you?

SHADOW: Understand we have no other way out. On the one hand there are we three, and on the other the cabinet ministers, the Privy Councilors, all the officials in the kingdom, the police and the army. We won't win in a pitched battle. Believe me, I was always closer to the earth than you. Listen to me: this scrap of paper will pacify them. This evening you'll hire a carriage, no one will follow you. And in the forest we—the princess and I—will get in the carriage with you. And in a few hours we'll be free. Understand, —free. Here's a portable inkwell, here's the quill. Sign it.

SCHOLAR: All right then. The princess will be here any minute and I'll consult with her, and if there's no other way out, I'll sign.

SHADOW: You mustn't wait! The Prime Minister gave me twenty minutes flat. He doesn't believe you can be bought, he considers our discussion a mere formality. The murderers on duty are already sitting outside his office, awaiting orders. Sign.

SCHOLAR: It rubs me the wrong way.

SHADOW: Are you a murderer too? Refusing to sign this paltry little scrap of paper, you're killing me, more than a friend to you, and the poor helpless princess. We won't survive your death!

SCHOLAR: All right, all right. Hand it over, I'll sign it. But only... Never again in my life will I ever come anywhere near a palace... (Signs the paper)

SHADOW: And here's the royal seal. (Impresses the seal.)

(GIULIA runs on. The SHADOW modestly withdraws to one side.)

GIULIA: Christian! I'm ruined.

SCHOLAR: What's happened?

GIULIA: Please help me.

SCHOLAR: Of course... But how? Are you joking?

GIULIA: No! Is it because I'm smiling? That's out of habit. Come with me at once. Let's go!

SCHOLAR: Word of honor, I can't leave this spot. The princess will be here any minute.

GIULIA: It's a matter of life or death!

SCHOLAR: Ah, I can imagine what the matter is... You've learned from the Finance Minister the trouble

lying in wait for me, and want to warn me. Thank you,
Giulia, but...

GIULIA: Ah, you don't understand... Well, stay
here then. No! I don't want to be a well-meaning,
sentimental housewife. I have no intention of warning
you. This matter is about me! Christian, forgive me...
Come with me, otherwise I shall perish. Do you want
me to go on my knees to you? Let's go!

SCHOLAR: All right. I'll just have a few words with my
friend. (*Walks over to the* SHADOW) Listen, the princess
will be here any minute.

SHADOW: Yes.

SCHOLAR: Tell her that I'll be back in a flash. I can't say
no to this woman. Something bad has happened.

SHADOW: Don't worry. I'll explain it all to the princess.

SCHOLAR: Thanks. (*He exits.*)

SHADOW: Damned force of habit! My arms, legs, neck
are aching. I kept wanting to imitate his movements.
It's simply dangerous... (*Opens the file folder.*) There...
Item four—taken care of... (*Becomes enrapt in reading.*)

(*Enter the* PRINCESS *and the* PRIVY COUNCILOR. *The*
SHADOW *straightens up and looks fixedly at the* PRINCESS.)

PRINCESS: Privy Councilor, where is he? Why isn't he
here?

PRIVY COUNCILOR: (*In a whisper*) He'll be here any
minute, princess, and all will be well.

PRINCESS: No, this is a terrible disaster! Be quiet, you
understand nothing about it. You aren't in love, it's
easy for you to say all will be well! And besides, I'm a
princess, I don't know how to wait. What's that music?

PRIVY COUNCILOR: It's in the restaurant, princess.

PRINCESS: Why do they always play music in our restaurants?

PRIVY COUNCILOR: So they can't hear people chewing, princess.

PRINCESS: Leave me in peace... What's that now? *(To the* SHADOW.*)* Hey, you, why are you staring at me with those big eyes.

SHADOW: I have to have a word with you and I don't dare, princess.

PRINCESS: Just who are you?

SHADOW: I'm his best friend.

PRINESS. Whose?

SHADOW: I am the best friend of the man you're waiting for, princess.

PRINCESS: Really? Why don't you say something?

SHADOW: My answer may seem insolent, princess.

PRINCESS: Never mind, speak out.

SHADOW: I hold my tongue because your beauty has struck me dumb.

PRINCESS: But that's not insolence. He sent you to me?

SHADOW: Yes. He asked me to say that he will be here any minute, princess. He's being detained by most important business. All is well, princess.

PRINCESS: But he'll be here soon?

SHADOW: Yes.

PRINCESS: Well, I'm in a good mood again. You shall amuse me until he shows up. Won't you?

(The SHADOW *remains silent.)*

PRINCESS: Well! It's awkward for me to have to remind you that I am a princess. I am used to people amusing me.

SHADOW: All right, I shall carry out your command. I will tell you dreams, princess.

PRINCESS: Are your dreams interesting?

SHADOW: I will tell you your dreams, princess.

PRINCESS: Mine?

SHADOW: Yes. The day before yesterday you dreamed that the walls of the palace had turned into ocean waves. You cried out: "Christian!" —and he showed up in a boat and reached out his hand to you.

PRINCESS: But I never told that dream to anyone!

SHADOW: And you found yourself in a forest... And a wolf suddenly rose up out of the shrubbery. And Christian said, "Don't be afraid, it's a good wolf" — and petted it. And there's another dream as well. You were galloping across a field on a charger. The grass in your path kept growing higher and higher and finally became a wall all around. It seemed to you to be beautiful, wonderfully beautiful, so beautiful that you began to weep and woke up in tears.

PRINCESS: But how come you know this?

SHADOW: Love can do miracles, princess.

PRINCESS: Love?

SHADOW: Yes. I am a very unhappy man, princess. I love you.

PRINCESS: Is that so...Councilor!

PRIVY COUNCILOR: Yes, princess.

PRINCESS: Call... No, move five paces away.

(The PRIVY COUNCILOR counts five paces.)

PRINCESS: I...

SHADOW: You wanted him to call the guard, princess, and, not understanding how this happened, you ordered him to move five paces away.

PRINCESS: You...

SHADOW: I love you, princess. And you feel it yourself. I am so filled with you that I understand your soul as I do my own. I told you only two of your dreams, but I remember them all. I know even your scary dreams, and the funny ones, and the ones that can only be whispered in your ear.

PRINCESS: No...

SHADOW: Do you want me to tell you the dream that stunned you? Remember? In that dream it is not he, not Christian who was with you, but quite a different man with an unfamiliar face, and that was exactly what you liked. You being with him...

PRINCESS: Councilor! Summon the guard.

PRIVY COUNCILOR: Right away, princess.

PRINCESS: But have the guard stand over there, behind the shrubbery for a while. Keep talking. I am listening, because...because it's simply too boring to wait for him.

SHADOW: People don't know the shadowy side of things, but it's just there in the shadows, in the half-light, in the depths that what gives edge to our feelings is lurking. In the depths of your soul am I.

PRINCESS: That'll do. I've suddenly come to my senses! The guards will arrest you now, and by nightfall you'll be headless.

SHADOW: Read this!

(The SHADOW takes from the folder the paper the SCHOLAR signed. The PRINCESS reads it.)

SHADOW: He's a dear man, a lovely man, but he's petty. He convinced you to run away with him because he was afraid to be a king—it's too dangerous. And he betrayed you. Coward!

PRINCESS: I don't believe this paper.

SHADOW: But here's the royal seal. I bought off your insignificant fiancé, I took you by force. Order them to cut off my head.

PRINCESS: You don't give me a chance to recover. How do I know, perhaps you don't love me either. What an unhappy girl I am!

SHADOW: What about the dreams? You've forgot the dreams, princess. How did I know your dreams? Only love can bring about such a miracle.

PRINCESS: Ah, yes, that's true...

SHADOW: Farewell, princess.

PRINCESS: You...you're going? ...How dare you! Come over here, give me your hand... This... All this... is so... so interesting... *(Kiss)* I...I don't even know your name.

SHADOW: Theodor-Christian.

PRINCESS: How nice! It's almost...almost the same. *(Kiss)*

(The SCHOLAR *runs in and stops short.)*

PRIVY COUNCILOR: I advise you to leave this place, the princess is granting audience here to one of her subjects.

SCHOLAR: Louisa!

PRINCESS: Go away, you petty man.

SCHOLAR: What are you saying, Louisa?

PRINCESS: You signed a paper in which you turned me down?

SCHOLAR: Yes...but...

PRINCESS: That'll do. You are a nice man, but you're a nonentity! Let's go, Theodor-Christian, my dear.

SCHOLAR: Villain! *(Rushes at the* SHADOW*)*

PRINCESS: Guard!

(The GUARD *springs out of the shrubbery.)*

PRINCESS: Escort us to the palace.

(They exit. The SCHOLAR *drops on to a bench. The* DOCTOR *hurries in from the gazebo.)*

DOCTOR: Wave your hand to dismiss it all. Wave your hand this very minute or you'll go out of your mind.

SCHOLAR: Do you know what just happened?

DOCTOR: Yes, I have very sensitive hearing. I heard it all.

SCHOLAR: How did he manage to get her to kiss him?

DOCTOR: He stunned her. He told her all her dreams.

SCHOLAR: How did he know her dreams?

DOCTOR: Dreams and shadows are closely related. I believe they're cousins...

SCHOLAR: You heard it all and didn't interfere?

DOCTOR: Are you joking! After all he's the Official for Top Priority Cases. Have you no idea of how awesome that power is? ...I knew a man of extraordinary courage. He went after bears with a knife, once he even went after a lion with his bare hands, —true, he never came back from that last hunt. And that very man fell into a faint, having accidentally jostled a Privy Councilor. It's a special kind of terror. Is it so wonderful that I am afraid of him too? No, I didn't interfere, and you will wave your hand to dismiss it all.

SCHOLAR: I won't.

DOCTOR: But what can you do?

SCHOLAR: I shall destroy him.

DOCTOR: No. Listen to me, you have no idea, no one on earth has any idea of the great discovery I have made. I have found the source of carbonated water of life. It's not far from here. Near the palace itself. This water cures all diseases on earth and even revives the dead, if they're good people. And what has come of it? The Finance Minister ordered me to seal up the source. If we were to cure all the sick, who would need us doctors? I fought with the minister like a maniac—and then the officials moved in on me. None of it mattered to them. Life and death and great discoveries. And that's the very reason they overcame me. So I waved my hand to dismiss it all. And all at once it became easier for me to live in this world. So you wave your hand at it all and go on living as I do.

SCHOLAR: Living for what? For the sake of what?

DOCTOR: Ah, lots of things... There, a patient's been cured. There, the wife's gone away for the weekend. There, I read in the paper that somehow I've given them hope.

SCHOLAR: Is that all?

DOCTOR: But you want to live so you can make more people happy? You think the officials will let you live? The people themselves can't stand it. Wave your hand at them. Look through your fingers at that insane, unhappy world.

SCHOLAR: I can't.

(Trumpets and drums offstage)

DOCTOR: He's coming back. (Rapidly exits into the gazebo)

(A great detachment of Guards *with* Trumpeters *and* Drummers *appears. It is headed by the* Shadow *in a black tailcoat and dazzling linen. The procession halts center stage.)*

Shadow: Christian! I'll give two or three orders and then deal with you!

(The Prime Minister *runs in, huffing and puffing. The* Lackeys *run in on the double, carrying the* Finance Minister. Pietro *and* Cesare Borgia *appear arm in arm.)*

Prime Minister: What's the meaning of this! We've made our decision.

Shadow: But I remade the decision on my own.

Prime Minister: Now listen here…

Shadow: No, you listen here, my good man. Do you know whom you're talking to?

Prime Minister: Yes.

Shadow: Then why don't you call me "your excellency"? Weren't you at the Head Office?

Prime Minister: No, I was having dinner, your excellency.

Shadow: Go back to it. Case No. 8989 is closed. Filed at the end are the princess's commands and my order No. 0001. There it is ordered that I be called "your excellency" until such time as we come up with a new, appropriate title.

Prime Minister: So, that means it's all formalized?

Shadow: Yes.

Prime Minister: Then nothing's to be done. Congratulations, your excellency.

Shadow: Why so glum, Finance Minister?

FINANCE MINISTER: I don't know how this will be greeted in financial circles. All the same you're of the breed of scholars. All sorts of changes will be set in motion, and we can't stand it.

SHADOW: No changes at all. As it was, so it will be. No plans at all. No prospects at all. That's the latest conclusion of my scholarship.

FINANCE MINISTER: In that case congratulations, your excellency.

SHADOW: Pietro! The princess has chosen a fiancé, but it's not you.

PIETRO: He can go to hell, your excellency, just pay me.

SHADOW: Cesare Borgia! You will not be king either.

CESARE BORGIA: All that's left for me—is to write my memoirs, your excellency.

SHADOW: Don't be downhearted. I value old friends, who knew me when I was a mere Official for Top Priority Cases. You are appointed royal secretary. You—captain of the royal guard.

(PIETRO *and* CESARE BORGIA *bow.*)

SHADOW: Gentlemen, you are dismissed.

(*Everyone exits, bowing. The* SHADOW *walks over to the* SCHOLAR.)

SHADOW: You saw that?

SCHOLAR: Yes.

SHADOW: What do you have to say to it?

SCHOLAR: I say: make haste to give up the princess and the throne—or I shall make you do it.

SHADOW: Listen, you insignificant fellow. Tomorrow I shall issue a whole series of orders—and you will turn out to be one man against the whole world. Friends will turn away from you in disgust. Enemies will laugh in your face. And you will come crawling to me and beg for mercy.

SCHOLAR: No.

SHADOW: We shall see. At twelve o'clock midnight between Tuesday and Wednesday you will come to the palace and send me a note: "I give up, Christian-Theodor." And I, so be it, will grant you a position near my person. Guards, follow me!

(Trumpets and drums. The SHADOW *exits with his entourage.)*

SCHOLAR: Annunciata! Annunciata!

*(*ANNUNCIATA *runs in.)*

ANNUNCIATA: I'm here. Sir! Maybe... maybe you'll follow doctor's orders? Maybe, you'll wave your hand at it all? Forgive me... Don't be mad at me. I'll help you. I'll be useful to you. I'm a very loyal girl, sir.

SCHOLAR: Annunciata, this fairy tale is very depressing!

(Curtain)

END OF ACT TWO

ACT THREE

Scene 1

(Night. Torches are ablaze. Lamps of colored glass are burning on the cornices, columns and balconies of the palace. A crowd, lively and noisy.)

VERY TALL LANKY MAN: Who wants to hear me tell what I see? All for two groschen. Who wants to hear? Oh, it's so interesting!

SHORT MAN: Don't listen to him. Listen to me, I can creep in everywhere, I know it all. Who wants to hear the news, all for two groschen? The way they met, how they got acquainted, how the ex-fiancé got his walking papers.

1ST WOMAN: We've been told the ex-fiancé was a very nice man!

2ND WOMAN: Not a bit of it! Very nice! He turned her down for a cool million.

1ST WOMAN: What? Where'd you get that?

2ND WOMAN: Everybody knows about it! She says to him: "You nutcase, if you was king you'd be makin' more than that!" And he says, "What, and have to work for it?"

1ST WOMAN: Folks like that should be drowned!

2ND WOMAN: Too true! It's too hard for him to be king. He should try housework!

VERY TALL LANKY MAN: Who wants me to tell what I
see through the window: the leader of the royal lackeys
is walking down the corridor and...well, who wants to
know what comes next? All for two groschen.

SHORT MAN: Who wants a portrait of the new king?
Life-size! With the crown on his head! With a sweet
smile on his lips. With kindliness in his eyes!

1ST MAN IN THE CROWD: Now there's a king, life will
be much better.

2ND MAN IN THE CROWD: Why's that?

1ST MAN IN THE CROWD: I'll explain right away. You
see?

2ND MAN IN THE CROWD: What?

1ST MAN IN THE CROWD: You see who's standing
there?

2ND MAN IN THE CROWD: Looks like the captain of the
guard?

1ST MAN IN THE CROWD: Why, that's him, in disguise.

2ND MAN IN THE CROWD: Aha, I see. (At the top of
his lungs) Now we've got a king, we'll start to live.
(Quietly) He may be in disguise, but his feet are in
army boots with spurs. (Loudly) Oh, how my heart
rejoices!

1ST MAN IN THE CROWD: (At the top of his lungs) Sure,
what kind of a life is it without a king! We were simply
pining for one!

CROWD: All hail our new king. Theodor the First!
Hurrah!

(They disperse, little by little, with anxious glances at
PIETRO. He remains alone. The figure of a man in a cloak
detaches itself from the wall.)

PIETRO: Well, what's new, Corporal?

CORPORAL: Nothing, all's quiet. Two arrests have been made.

PIETRO: What for?

CORPORAL: One man instead of shouting "All hail the King" shouted "All hail the Thing".

PIETRO: And the other?

CORPORAL: The other is my neighbor.

PIETRO: What did he do?

CORPORAL: Nothing in particular. He's got a nasty temper. He called my wife a "pumpkin". I've had it in for him for a long time now. And how're things with you, Captain?

PIETRO: All's quiet. The people are jubilating.

CORPORAL: Allow me to point out, Captain sir. The boots.

PIETRO: What boots?

CORPORAL: You forgot to change your boots again. The spurs on them jingle.

PIETRO: So what? It's an occasion!

CORPORAL: The people will figure out who you are. You see how it's emptied out around here?

PIETRO: Yes... However... You're one of us, I can tell you the truth: I wear boots with spurs on purpose.

CORPORAL: That can't be right!

PIETRO: Yes. It's better to let them know I'm coming, otherwise you'd get such an earful you won't sleep three nights running.

CORPORAL: Yes, that may be.

PIETRO: With boots things're much quieter. You walk around, you jingle your spurs—and all you hear around you is what's proper.

CORPORAL: Yes, that's true.

PIETRO: It's easy for them, there at the Head Office. They only have to deal with documents. But how am I supposed to handle the people?

CORPORAL: Yes, the people…

PIETRO *(In a whisper.)* You know, I tell you what: the people does what it wants!

CORPORAL: You don't say so!

PIETRO: Take it from me. In there the sovereign is celebrating the coronation, a gala wedding of the biggest celebrities is on the cards, and what are the people up to? Lots of lads and lasses are kissing two paces away from the palace, after picking out the darkest corners. In house number eight the tailor's wife decided to have a baby this very minute. Such a major event going on in the kingdom, but it makes no never mind to her, she goes on howling! The old blacksmith in house number three up and died. Festivities at court, and he lies in a coffin and doesn't give a good goddam. It's chaos!

CORPORAL: Which room is giving birth? I'll fine it.

PIETRO: That's not the point, Corporal. It scares me, the way they dare to behave. How's that for obstinacy, Corporal? And suddenly just as quietly, obstinately, all at once they… What're you up to?

CORPORAL: Nothing…

PIETRO: Look here, pal… How're you standin'?

(The CORPORAL stands to attention.)

PIETRO: I got your numberrr! Old bastard… You're gettin' out o' hand! You're usin' your brain! Pleased to meet you, Voltaire Rousseau! What time is it?

CORPORAL: A quarter to twelve, Captain sir.

PIETRO: You rec'llect what you're to call out at the stroke of midnight?

CORPORAL: Yes sir, Captain sir.

PIETRO: I'm goin' to the Head Office, have a lie-down, enjoy the quiet, read different sorts o' documents, while you stay here and announce what you're supposed to, don't forget! *(Exits)*

(The SCHOLAR *appears.)*

SCHOLAR: I'm very pleased that these lamps are burning. I feel as if never in my life has my brain worked so clearly. I see all these lamps as a totality, and each little lamp in particular. I know that you'll flicker out in the morning, my friends, but that doesn't bother you. You go on burning just the same, and burning merrily, -- no one can take that away from you.

DOCTOR: *(Muffled up from head to foot)* Christian!

SCHOLAR: Who's that! Why, it's the Doctor.

DOCTOR: You recognized me so easily... *(Glances around)* Let's step over to the side. Turn away from me! No, I've got a jingling in my ears, and I thought it was spurs. Don't be angry. After all I've got such a big family.

SCHOLAR: I'm not angry.

(The DOCTOR *and thhe* SCHOLAR *come down to the forestage.)*

DOCTOR: Tell me as your doctor have you decided to give in?

SCHOLAR: No. My conscience is clear, I have to go and tell them what I know.

DOCTOR: But that's suicide.

SCHOLAR: Possibly.

DOCTOR: I beg of you, give in.

SCHOLAR: I cannot.

DOCTOR: They'll cut off your head!

SCHOLAR: I don't believe it. On one hand, a living life, on the other a shadow. Everything I know tells me that the shadow can prevail for only a while. But the world is sustained by us, by the people who do the work! Farewell!

DOCTOR: Listen, people get vicious when you go against them. But if you live in peace with them, they can seem to be all right.

SCHOLAR: Is that what you wanted to tell me?

DOCTOR: No! Maybe I'm out of my mind, but I can't watch you go in there unarmed. Hush. Remember these words "Shadow, know your place."

SCHOLAR: I don't understand you!

DOCTOR: These last few days I've been rummaging in ancient writings about people who have lost their shadows. In one research paper the author, an eminent professor, recommends this formula: the shadow's owner must shout at it: "Shadow, know your place," and then it will, for a time, turn back into a shadow.

SCHOLAR: What are you saying! Why, that's wonderful! Everyone will be able to see that he's a shadow. So there! I told you he'd come to a bad end! Life is against him. We...

DOCTOR: Leave me out of it... Farewell. (*Exits quickly*)

SCHOLAR: Very good. I thought I'd perish with honor, but to prevail is even better. They shall see that he's a shadow and they'll understand... Well, in short, they'll understand it all...I...

(*A crowd of people runs in.*)

SCHOLAR: What's happened?

1ST MAN: The corporal is coming here with a bugle.

SCHOLAR: Why?

1ST MAN: He's going to announce something... Here he is... Hush...

CORPORAL: Christian-Theodor! Christian-Theodor!

SCHOLAR: What is it? I think I'm losing my nerve!

CORPORAL: Christian-Theodor! Christian-Theodor!

SCHOLAR: *(Loudly)* Here I am.

CORPORAL: Do you have a letter for the king?

SCHOLAR: Here it is.

CORPORAL: Follow me!

(Curtain)

Scene II

(An audience chamber in the royal palace. The COURTIERS *are sitting around in groups. Subdued conversations.* MAJOR-DOMO *and* AIDES *hand around refreshments on trays.)*

1ST COURTIER: *(Gray hair, handsome, lugubrious expression.)* They used to serve the ice cream in the shape of charming little lambs, or rabbits, or kittens. The blood would freeze in your veins whenever you bit off the head of such a cute, innocent creature.

1ST LADY: Yes indeed! The blood used to freeze in my veins too, ice cream is so cold!

1ST COURTIER: Nowadays they serve the ice cream in the shape of beautiful fruits—it's much more humane.

1ST LADY: Right you are! What a tender heart you have. How are your dear canary-birds getting on?

1ST COURTIER: Ah, one of them, Golden Droplet by name, caught a cold and coughed so that I almost fell ill myself out of sympathy. She's much better now. She is even trying to sing, but I won't allow it.

(Enter PIETRO.)

PIETRO: Greetings! What are you eating there, gentlemen?

2ND COURTIER: Ice cream, Captain of the Royal Guard, sir.

PIETRO: Hey! Give me a portion. On the double, damn it! Don't be stingy, you bastard!

2ND COURTIER: Are you that fond of ice cream, Captain, sir.

PIETRO: I hate it. But if they're handin' it out, you gotta get some, damn it to hell!

MAJOR-DOMO: Pastries filled with rose-flavored custard! Would you like some, courtiers, sirs and madams? *(Quietly to the LACKEYS)* First the dukes, then the counts, then the barons. Dukes six pastries apiece, counts four, barons two, the rest whatever's left. Don't get it mixed up.

ONE OF THE LACKEYS: But how many pastries do we give the new royal secretaries?

MAJOR-DOMO: Six and a half.

(Enter CESARE BORGIA.)

CESARE BORGIA: Greetings, ladies and gentlemen. Look at me. Well? How about it? How do you like my cravat, ladies and gentlemen? This cravat is more than fashionable. It won't be in fashion till two weeks from now..

3RD COURTIER: But how did you manage to obtain this masterpiece?

CESARE BORGIA: Oh, quite simply. My cravat purveyor is an admiral of the royal fleet. He imports cravats for me from abroad and smuggles them ashore in his three-cornered hat.

3RD COURTIER: How brilliantly simple!

CESARE BORGIA: As royal secretary, I will order you a dozen cravats. Ladies and gentlemen, I want to delight you. May I? Then follow me, I will show you my apartments. Mahogany, Chinese porcelain. Would you like to take a peek?

COURTIERS: Of course! We're dying with impatience! How kind of you, Royal Secretary, sir.

(CESARE BORGIA *exits, followed by the* COURTIERS. ANNUNCIATA *enters, followed by* GIULIA.)

GIULIA: Annunciata! Are you angry with me? Don't deny it! Now that you're the daughter of a dignitary I can read quite clearly in your face—you're angry with me. Aren't you?

ANNUNCIATA: Ah, actually it's not on my mind, madam.

GIULIA: So *he's* still on your mind? The scholar?

ANNUNCIATA: Yes.

GIULIA: You can't possibly think that he can prevail?

ANNUNCIATA: I don't care.

GIULIA: You're wrong. You're still a little girl. You don't know that the real man is the one who prevails... Only it's terrible that you can never identify for sure who will prevail in the end. Christian-Theodor is so peculiar! Do you know anything about him?

ANNUNCIATA: Oh, this is such a disaster! They've moved us to court, and Papa ordered the lackeys not to let me out. I can't even send a letter to Mister Scholar. And he probably thinks that I have abandoned him. Cesare Borgia runs him down in the newspaper every day, papa reads it and drools over it, while I read it and almost start to cry. Just now in the corridor I bumped into that Cesare Borgia and didn't even apologize.

GIULIA: He didn't notice, believe me.

ANNUNCIATA: Perhaps. Do you know anything about Mister Scholar, madam?

GIULIA: Yes. I do. My friends the cabinet ministers tell me everything. Christian-Theodor is now totally isolated. And, despite it all, he walks around smiling.

ANNUNCIATA: How awful!

GIULIA: Of course. Who behaves like that under such oppressive conditions? It's incomprehensible. I have arranged my life so smoothly, so elegantly, and now suddenly—I'm almost suffering. Suffering is not at all pleasant! *(Laughs out loud flirtatiously)*

ANNUNCIATA: What's come over you, madam?

GIULIA: The courtiers are coming back. Mister Minister, there you are at last! I was really missing you. Greetings!

(The LACKEYS *bring in the* FINANCE MINISTER.*)*

FINANCE MINISTER: One, two, three, four... Right. All the diamonds in place. One, two, three... And the pearls. And the rubies. Greetings, Giulia! Where have you been?...

GIULIA: Ah, your proximity excites me too much... The world might take notice...

FINANCE MINISTER: But our relationship has been formalized by decree...

GIULIA: It doesn't matter...I shall go. That will be much more elegant. *(Goes away)*

FINANCE MINISTER: She is an honest-to-god goddess…
Lackeys! Seat me against the wall. Put me in the pose
of complete satisfaction with the turn of events. Step
lively!

(The LACKEYS *carry out their orders.)*

FINANCE MINISTER: Begone!

(The LACKEYS *exit. The* PRIME MINISTER, *as if strolling,
approaches the* FINANCE MINISTER.*)*

FINANCE MINISTER: *(Smiling, quietly.)* How are things,
Mister Prime Minister?

PRIME MINISTER: Everything seems to be in order.
(Smiles.)

FINANCE MINISTER: What do you mean, seems?

PRIME MINISTER: After my long years in office I have
discovered a not very pleasant law. No sooner have we
fully triumphed, when life rears its head.

FINANCE MINISTER: Rears its head? …I hope you've
summoned the royal headsman?

PRIME MINISTER: Yes, he's here. Smile, they're watching
us.

FINANCE MINISTER: *(Smiles)* And the axe and the block?

PRIME MINISTER: In place. The block is set up in the
pink drawing-room, near the statue of Cupid, and
camouflaged with forget-me-nots.

FINANCE MINISTER: What can the Scholar do?

PRIME MINISTER: Nothing. He is isolated and
powerless. But these honest, naïve people sometimes
act so unpredictably!

FINANCE MINISTER: Why wasn't he executed at once?

PRIME MINISTER: The king is against it. Smile! *(He moves
away, smiling.)*

(Enter the PRIVY COUNCILOR.*)*

PRIVY COUNCILOR: Courtiers, ladies and gentlemen, I greet you! His Majesty and his most august bride are directing their steps to this audience chamber. Oh be joyful.

(Everyone rises. The door is flung wide open. Enter arm in arm the SHADOW *and the* PRINCESS.*)*

SHADOW: *(With an elegant and majestic wave of the hand)* Be seated!

COURTIERS: *(In chorus)* We won't.

SHADOW: Be seated!

COURTIERS: We daren't.

SHADOW: Be seated!

COURTIERS: Well, so be it. *(They sit.)*

PRIME MINISTER: I am here, your majesty!

SHADOW: What time is it?

PRIME MINISTER: A quarter to twelve, your majesty!

SHADOW: You may go.

PRINCESS: Where are we, which audience chamber?

SHADOW: The lesser throne room, Princess. You see?

PRINCESS: I see nothing but you. I don't recognize the rooms in which I grew up, the people with whom I've lived so many years. I would like to fling it all away and stay with you.

SHADOW: So would I.

PRINCESS: Something is on your mind?

SHADOW: Yes, I promised to pardon Christian if he came here at midnight tonight. He's a loser, but I've been friends with him for so many years…

PRINCESS: How can you think of anybody but me? After all, our wedding is in an hour.

SHADOW: But we met thanks to Christian!

PRINCESS: Ah, yes. What a good man you are, Theodor! Yes, we shall pardon him. He's a loser, but you have been friends with him for so many years...

SHADOW: Privy Councilor!

PRIVY COUNCILOR: Here I am, your majesty!

SHADOW: A man will be here shortly, with whom I wish to speak in private.

PRIVY COUNCILOR: Yes, your majesty! Courtiers, ladies and gentlemen! His majesty is pleased to grant an audience in this chamber to one of his subjects. Oh lucky fellow!

(The COURTIERS *rise and bow their way out.)*

PRINCESS: You think he'll come?

SHADOW: What else can he do? *(Kisses the* PRINCESS'*s hand.)* I'll call you as soon as I have comforted and pacified him.

PRINCESS: I'm off, dearest. What a remarkable man you are! *(Exits following the* COURTIERS.*)*

(The SHADOW *opens a window. He listens in. A clock chimes in the next room.)*

SHADOW: Midnight. He'll be here any minute now.

(In the far distance, down below, the CORPORAL *shouts.)*

CORPORAL: Christian-Theodor! Christian-Theodor!

SHADOW: What's that? I feel I'm losing my nerve...

CORPORAL: Christian-Theodor! Christian-Theodor?!

SCHOLAR: *(Off)* Here I am.

CORPORAL: Do you have a letter for the king?

SCHOLAR: Here it is.

CORPORAL: Follow me!

SHADOW: *(Slams the window shut, goes to the throne, sits on it.)* I can crawl at length along the floor, climb up a wall and drop through a window, all at the same time, —is he capable of such agility? I can lie on the roadway and pedestrians, wagon wheels, horses' hooves can't do me the slightest harm—could he so adapt himself to a locale? In the past two weeks I've learned about life a thousand times better than he could. Inaudibly, like a shadow, I penetrated everywhere, and peered and eavesdropped and read other people's letters. I know the whole shadowy side of things. And now here I am sitting on the throne, and he lies at my feet.

(The door opens wide, the CAPTAIN OF THE GUARD *enters.)*

PIETRO: A letter, your majesty.

SHADOW: Give it here. *(Reads)* "I have come. Christian-Theodor." Where is he?

PIETRO: Outside the door, your majesty.

SHADOW: Show him in.

(The CAPTAIN OF THE GUARD *exits. The* SCHOLAR *appears. He stands facing the throne.)*

SHADOW: Well, how are things, Christian-Theodor?

SCHOLAR: Things are looking bad for me, Theodor-Christian.

SHADOW: How so?

SCHOLAR: I suddenly find myself completely isolated.

SHADOW: But what of your friends?

SCHOLAR: They believe slanders about me.

SHADOW: And where is that girl who loved you?

SCHOLAR: She is now your bride.

SHADOW: Whose fault is that, Christian-Theodor?

SCHOLAR: It's your fault, Theodor-Christian.

SHADOW: Now that's a genuine conversation between a man and his shadow. Privy Councilor!

(The PRIVY COUNCILOR *runs in.)*

SHADOW: Everyone in here! Quick as they can!

(Enter the PRINCESS, *sits beside the* SHADOW. COURTIERS *enter and stand all around. In their midst the* DOCTOR.*)*

SHADOW: Be seated!

COURTIERS: We won't!

SHADOW: Be seated!

COURTIERS: We daren't!

SHADOW: Be seated!

COURTIERS: Well, so be it! *(They sit.)*

SHADOW: Ladies and gentlemen, before you stands a man whom I should like to make happy. For his whole life he's been a loser. Finally, luckily for him, I ascended to the throne. I appoint him my shadow. Congratulate him, ladies and gentlemen of the court!

(The COURTIERS *rise and bow.)*

SHADOW: I raise him to the same rank and honors as a royal secretary.

MAJOR-DOMO: *(In a loud whisper)* **Prepare six and a half pastries for him!**

SHADOW: Don't be embarrassed, Christian-Theodor! If at first you find it difficult, I shall give you a few good lessons, the same sort you've had these last few days. And soon you will turn into a genuine shadow, Christian-Theodor. Take your place at our feet.

PRIME MINISTER: Your majesty, his appointment has not yet been made official. Allow me to order the Captain of the Guard to take him away until tomorrow.

SHADOW: No! Christian-Theodor! Take your place at our feet.

SCHOLAR: Not for the world! Ladies and gentlemen! Listen seriously to my serious words! This is the real shadow. My shadow! A shadow has seized the throne. You hear me?

PRIME MINISTER: I knew it. Majesty!

SHADOW: *(Calmly)* Hush, prime minister! Speak, loser! I shall admire the very last failure in your life.

SCHOLAR: Princess, I never refused your hand. He tricked and confused both of us.

PRINCESS: I will not discuss it!

SCHOLAR: But you wrote to me that you were ready to leave the palace and go away with me wherever I wanted.

PRINCESS: I will not, will not, will not discuss it!

SCHOLAR: But I came here for you, princess. Give me your hand—and let's run away. To be the wife of a shadow means turning into an ugly, spiteful frog.

PRINCESS: What you are saying is most unpleasant. Why should I listen to you?

SCHOLAR: Louisa!

PRINCESS: My lips are sealed!

SCHOLAR: Ladies and gentlemen!

PRIVY COUNCILOR: I counsel you not to listen to him. Really educated people simply do not pay attention to uneducated people.

SCHOLAR: Ladies and gentlemen! This cruel creature is destroying you all. He has attained the highest power, but he's empty. He's already languishing and doesn't know what to do with himself. And he'll start tormenting you all out of boredom and idleness.

1ST COURTIER: My little wood lark eats out of my hand. And my little starling calls me "papa."

SCHOLAR: Giulia! We were such friends, you must know who I am. Tell them.

FINANCE MINISTER: Giulia, I adore you, but if you speak out of turn, I'll grind you into dust.

SCHOLAR: Giulia, tell them.

GIULIA: *(Points at the* SCHOLAR*)* The shadow is you!

SCHOLAR: How can I be talking in a wilderness!

ANNUNCIATA: No, no! Father is always threatening to kill you, that's why I've kept silent. Ladies and gentlemen, listen to me! *(Points at the* SHADOW*)* That's the shadow! Word of honor!

(Slight movement among the COURTIERS.*)*

ANNUNCIATA: I saw myself how he left Mister Scholar. I don't lie. The whole town knows I always tell the truth.

PIETRO: She cannot be a witness!

SCHOLAR: Why not?

PIETRO: She's in love with you.

SCHOLAR: Is that true, Annunciata?

ANNUNCIATA: Yes, forgive me for it. But all the same, listen to me, ladies and gentlemen.

SCHOLAR: That's enough, Annunciata. Thank you. Hey, you people! You didn't want to believe me, then believe your own eyes. Shadow! Know your place.

(The SHADOW *rises with difficulty, struggling with himself, walks over to the* SCHOLAR.*)*

PRIME MINISTER: Look! He's imitating all his movements. Help!

SCHOLAR: A shadow! He's simply a shadow! Are you a shadow, Theodor-Christian?

SHADOW: Yes, I'm a shadow, Christian-Theodor! Don't believe it! It's a lie! I order you to be executed!

SCHOLAR: You wouldn't dare, Theodor-Christian!

SHADOW: *(Falls)* I don't dare, Christian-Theodor!

PRIME MINISTER: That's enough! It's all clear to me now! This scholar is a madman! And his disease is contagious. The sovereign has fallen ill, but he will recover. Lackeys, take the sovereign away.

(The LACKEYS carry out the order. The PRINCESS runs after them.)

PRIME MINISTER: Guards!

(The CORPORAL enters with a detachment of SOLDIERS.)

PRIME MINISTER: Seize him!

(The SOLDIERS surround the SCHOLAR.)

PRIME MINISTER: Doctor!

(The DOCTOR steps out of the crowd of COURTIERS. The PRIME MINISTER points to the SCHOLAR.)

PRIME MINISTER: Is he insane?

DOCTOR: *(Waves his hand in dismissal)* I told him long ago that this was madness.

PRIME MINISTER: Is his madness contagious?

DOCTOR: Yes. I almost caught this madness myself.

PRIME MINISTER: Is it curable?

DOCTOR: No.

PRIME MINISTER: Which means, we must cut off his head.

PRIVY COUNCILOR: Allow me, Prime Minister, since I, as master of ceremonies, am in charge of the festivities.

PRIME MINISTER: Fine, fine!

PRIVY COUNCILOR: It would be crude, it would be inhumane to cut off the head of a poor madman. I protest against an execution, but a minor surgical procedure on the poor fellow's head should be performed at once.

PRIME MINISTER: Eloquently put.

PRIVY COUNCILOR: Our esteemed doctor, as everyone knows, is a therapist and not a surgeon. Therefore, in this specific case, in order to amputate the diseased organ, I recommend calling on the services of the royal headsman.

PRIME MINISTER: The royal headsman!

1ST COURTIER: Right this minute. *(Rises. Speaks to the lady beside him, while he puts on white gloves.)* Please forgive me. I'll be right back and then I'll tell you how I saved the life of my poor bunny. *(To the PRIME MINISTER)* I'm ready.

ANNUNCIATA: Let me say good-bye to him! Farewell, Christian-Theodor!

SCHOLAR: Farewell, Annunciata!

ANNUNCIATA: Are you terrified, Christian-Theodor?

SCHOLAR: Yes. But I won't beg for mercy. I...

PRIME MINISTER: Drum-roll!

PIETRO: Drum-roll!

(The DRUMMER beats a drum-roll.)

PRIME MINISTER: Forward march!

PIETRO: Forward march!

CORPORAL: Forward march!

(The CORPORAL *exits leading out the* SCHOLAR. *The* HEADSMAN *follows them.)*

PRIME MINISTER: Ladies and gentlemen, please step out on to the balcony and watch the fireworks. Meanwhile some cooling and refreshing beverages will be waiting for you here.

(Everyone rises, moves to go outside. On stage remain ANNUNCIATA *and* GIULIA.)

GIULIA: Annunciata, I couldn't act any other way. Forgive me.

ANNUNCIATA: He's in perfect health—and suddenly he has to die!

GIULIA: This is dreadfully, dreadfully unpleasant for me too, believe me. But what a scoundrel that doctor is! To betray his good friend that way!

ANNUNCIATA: What about you?

GIULIA: How can you compare us? That nobody of a doctor lost nothing by it. But I so love the stage. You're crying?

ANNUNCIATA: No. I'll cry at home in my room.

GIULIA: You have to learn how to clear your mind of everything that makes you suffer. A slight shake of the head—that's all there is to it. Like this. Try it.

ANNUNCIATA: I don't want to.

GIULIA: Don't turn away from me. I swear to you I'm ready to kill myself I'm so sorry. But that's between you and me.

ANNUNCIATA: Is he still alive?

GIULIA: Of course, of course! When it's all over, they'll beat the drums.

ANNUNCIATA: I don't believe that there's nothing to be done. I beg of you, Giulia, let's stop all this. We have to go there... Quickly!

GIULIA: Hush!

(The DOCTOR *hurries in.)*

DOCTOR: Wine!

MAJOR-DOMO: Wine for the Doctor!

GIULIA: Annunciata, if you give me your word you'll keep silent, I'll try to help you...

ANNUNCIATA: I won't say a word to anyone! Word of honor! Only hurry!

GIULIA: There's really no need to rush. My method can work only when it's all over. Be still. Listen closely. *(Walks over to the* DOCTOR*)* Doctor!

DOCTOR: Yes, Giulia.

GIULIA: I bet I know what's on your mind.

DOCTOR: Wine.

GIULIA: No, water...

DOCTOR: I'm in no mood for joking now, Giulia.

GIULIA: You know I'm not joking.

DOCTOR: Give me at least a moment to catch my breath.

GIULIA: Unfortunately, that's out of the question. Right now one of our mutual friends...well, in short, you understand me.

DOCTOR: What can I do?

GIULIA: How about the water?

DOCTOR: What water?

GIULIA: Remember the time when we were friends... Once the moon was shining down, the stars were twinkling, and you told me you had discovered the water of life, which cures all diseases and even raises the dead, if they had been good people.

ANNUNCIATA: Doctor, is that true? Is there such water?

DOCTOR: Giulia is joking, as always.

ANNUNCIATA: You're lying, I can see it. I'm going to kill you!

DOCTOR: I will be very pleased if you do.

ANNUNCIATA: Doctor, you will wake up tomorrow, but he will never wake up again. He called you his friend, his colleague!

DOCTOR: Stupid, unhappy little girl! What can I do? They keep all the water behind seven doors with seven locks, and the Finance Minister holds the keys.

GIULIA: I don't believe you didn't keep a bottle for yourself for a rainy day.

DOCTOR: No, Giulia! That's how honest I am. I didn't keep a single drop for myself, since I couldn't cure everyone.

GIULIA: You're not a man, you're a zero.

DOCTOR: After all, the Minister loves you, ask him for the keys, Giulia!

GIULIA: Me? Selfish fellow! He wants to foist all the blame on me.

ANNUNCIATA: Madam!

GIULIA: Not another word! I've done all I can.

ANNUNCIATA: Doctor!

DOCTOR: What can I do?

MAJOR-DOMO: His Majesty!

(The chamber fills with COURTIERS. *The* SHADOW *and the* PRINCESS *enter slowly. They sit on the throne. The* PRIME MINISTER *makes a sign to the* MAJOR-DOMO.*)*

MAJOR-DOMO: And now his Majesty's soprano soloist, who is under the protection of his excellency the honorable Finance Minister, Miss Giulia Giuli, will perform the cooling and refreshing ditty "It Doesn't Pay to Lose Your Head."

SHADOW: It's doesn't pay to lose your head... Beautiful!

GIULIA: *(Performs a low curtsey to the king. Bows to the courtiers. Sings.)*
A dragonfly lived in this land,
Who flirted with her eyes.
Their glance no creature could withstand,
And so flies died like flies.
There was one thing she often said:
It doesn't pay to lose your head...

(A thunderous drum-roll interrupts the song.)

SHADOW: *(Jumps up, staggering)* Water!

(The MAJOR-DOMO rushes to the SHADOW and stops in astonishment. The SHADOW's head suddenly flies off his shoulders. The headless SHADOW sits on the throne motionless.)

ANNUNCIATA: Look!

FINANCE MINISTER: What's going on?

PRIME MINISTER: Good heavens! We didn't figure on this. This must indeed be his own shadow. Ladies and gentlemen, you are at a party in the royal palace. You have to be merry, merry no matter what!

PRINCESS: *(Runs to the FINANCE MINISTER and the PRIME MINISTER)* Right now! Right now! Right now!

PRIME MINISTER: What, your highness?

PRINCESS: Right now restore him! I don't want this! Don't want this! Don't want this!

PRIME MINISTER: Princess, I beseech you, stop.

PRINCESS: Well, what would you say if your bridegroom lost his head?

PRIVY COUNCILOR: He did it for love, Princess.

PRINCESS: If you don't restore him, I will immediately order that your head be off. All the princesses in the world have intact husbands, but take a look at mine! What a dirty trick!...

PRIME MINISTER: The water of life, quick, quick, quick!

FINANCE MINISTER: For whom? For him? But it only revives good people.

PRIME MINISTER: We'll have to revive the good one. Not that I want to.

FINANCE MINISTER: There's no other way. Doctor! Follow me. Lackeys! Carry me! (*Exits.*)

PRIME MINISTER: Be calm, princess, everything possible will be done.

(1ST COURTIER *enters, removing his gloves. When he notices the headless king, he stops, frozen in place.*)

1ST COURTIER: If I may... But who did this? You step out of the room for half an hour—and somebody's pinched your job... It's a conspiracy!

(*The door is flung open, and a whole procession crosses the stage. First the* LACKEYS *carrying the* FINANCE MINISTER. *Behind him four* SOLDIERS *carry a big barrel. The barrel is glowing by itself. Tongues of flame lick out between the cracks. Shining drops fall on the polished parquet floor. The* DOCTOR *marches behind the barrel. The procession crosses the stage and disappears.*)

GIULIA: Annunciata, you were right.

ANNUNCIATA: About what?

GIULIA: He'll prevail! Now he'll prevail. They're bringing the water of life. It will revive him.

ANNUNCIATA: Why would they revive a good man?

GIULIA: So that the bad one can live. You should be happy, Annunciata.

ANNUNCIATA: I don't believe it, something else will happen, after all we're in the palace.

GIULIA: Ah, I'm afraid that nothing else will happen. Could it become fashionable—to be a good person? That will be such a headache!

CESARE BORGIA: Honorable Captain of the Royal Guard!

PIETRO: Now what?

CESARE BORGIA: The courtiers are giving us the stink-eye. Should we make a run for it?

PIETRO: Who the hell knows. They'll nab us!

CESARE BORGIA: We were allied with the loser.

PIETRO: I'll never forgive him, damn my eyes.

CESARE BORGIA: To lose his head at such a critical moment!

PIETRO: Nitwit! And in front of everyone too! He could have gone into his private office and lost it as much as he liked, the swine!

CESARE BORGIA: A tactless creature.

PIETRO: An ass!

CESARE BORGIA: No, we'll have to devour him. Have to, have to.

PIETRO: Yes, that's next.

(Thunderous drum-roll. The SHADOW's head suddenly reappears on his shoulders.)

CESARE BORGIA: Congratulations, your majesty.

PIETRO: Hurrah, your majesty.

MAJOR-DOMO: Some water, your majesty!

SHADOW: Why is this chamber so empty? Where is everybody? Louisa?

(The PRINCESS *runs in, followed by the* COURTIERS.*)*

PRINCESS: How well a head suits you, darling!

SHADOW: Louisa, where is he?

PRINCESS: I don't know. How are you feeling, dearest?

SHADOW: It hurts me to swallow.

PRINCESS: I'll make you a compress for over-night.

SHADOW: Thanks. But just where is he? Summon him here.

*(*FINANCE MINISTER *and* PRIME MINISTER *run in.)*

PRIME MINISTER: Splendid. Everything's in its place.

FINANCE MINISTER: No changes whatsoever!

PRIME MINISTER: Your majesty, do us a favor, nod your head.

SHADOW: Where is he?

PRIME MINISTER: Lovely! The head works! Hurrah! Everything's in order.

SHADOW: I'm asking you: where is he?

PRIME MINISTER: And I reply: everything is in order. He'll be locked up in a dungeon right this minute.

SHADOW: Have you gone out of your mind! How dare you even think about it! Guard of honor!

PIETRO: Guard of honor!

SHADOW: Go, beg, entreat him to come here.

PIETRO: Beg and entreat him—forward march!

*(*PIETRO *exits with the* HONOR GUARD.*)*

PRINCESS: Why are you summoning him, Theodor-Christian?

SHADOW: I want to live.

PRINCESS: But you said he's a loser.

SHADOW: And so he is, but I can't live without him!

(The DOCTOR *runs in.)*

DOCTOR: He has recovered. Listen to me, all of you: he behaved like a lunatic, walked straight ahead, without swerving, he was executed—and now he's alive, more alive than any of you.

MAJOR-DOMO: His radiance the Honorable Scholar.

(The SCHOLAR *enters. The* SHADOW *leaps up and extends his arms. The* SCHOLAR *ignores him.)*

SCHOLAR: Annunciata!

ANNUNCIATA: Here I am.

SCHOLAR: Annunciata, they didn't let me finish my speech. Yes, Annunciata. I was terrified of dying. After all, I'm so young!

SHADOW: Christian!

SCHOLAR: Shut up. But I went to my death, Annunciata. After all, in order to prevail, you have to go to your death. And now—I've prevailed. Let's leave here, Annunciata.

SHADOW: No! Stay with me, Christian. Live in the palace. Not a single hair of your head will be harmed. You want me to appoint you prime minister?

PRIME MINISTER: But why specifically prime? The Finance Minister is on his last legs.

FINANCE MINISTER: On my last legs? Look. *(Skips blithely around the room.)*

PRIME MINISTER: He's recovered!

FINANCE MINISTER: With us businessmen, a moment of real danger gives our feet wings.

SHADOW: You want me to banish them all, Christian? I'll let you rule—within reasonable limits, of course. I'll help you make a given number of people happy. You won't answer me? Louisa! Command him.

PRINCESS: Shut up, you coward! What have you done, ladies and gentlemen? Once in my life I met a good man, and you fell on him like hounds. Begone, get out of here, shadow!

(The SHADOW *slowly slips off the throne, adheres to the wall, muffled in a cloak.)*

PRINCESS: You can stand in the most pitiful pose you choose. You won't make me pity you. Ladies and gentlemen! He is no longer my fiancé. I shall find myself a new fiancé.

PRIVY COUNCILOR: O be joyful!

PRINCESS: I've understood it all, Christian, dearest. Hey! Captain of the Guard, seize him! *(Points to the* SHADOW*)*

PIETRO: As you will. Seize him! *(Goes to the* SHADOW*)*

PRIME MINISTER: I'll help you.

FINANCE MINISTER: So will I, so will I.

CESARE BORGIA: Down with the Shadow!

(They lay hold of the SHADOW*, but there is no* SHADOW*, the empty cloak hangs in their hands.)*

PRINCESS: He escaped...

SCHOLAR: He hid himself, so that from time to time he can be with me on the road. But I'll recognize him, I'll recognize him anywhere. Annunciata, give me your hand, let's get out of here.

ANNUNCIATA: How are you feeling, Christian-Theodor, my dear?

SCHOLAR: It hurts me to swallow. Farewell, ladies and gentlemen!

PRINCESS: Christian-Theodor, forgive me, I made a mistake for once in my life. Well, I'm already punished for it—and will be. Stay or take me with you. I will behave very nicely. You'll see.

SCHOLAR: No, Princess.

PRINCESS: Don't go. What an unhappy girl I am. Ladies and gentlemen, plead with him.

COURTIERS:

Where are you off to?

Stay here.

Sit down a while, please...

What's your hurry? It isn't bedtime yet.

SCHOLAR: Sorry, ladies and gentlemen, but I'm very busy.

(The SCHOLAR *takes* ANNUNCIATA *by the arm and starts to go.)*

PRINCESS: Christian-Theodor! It's raining outside. It's dark. But in the palace it's warm and cosy. I'll order them to stoke up all the stoves. Do stay.

SCHOLAR: No. We'll bundle up more warmly and go. Don't detain us, ladies and gentlemen.

CESARE BORGIA: Make way, make way! Here are your galoshes, Mister Professor!

PIETRO: Your lap rug. *(To* ANNUNCIATA*)* Put in a good word for your father, monster!

CORPORAL: The carriage is at the gate.

SCHOLAR: Annunciata, let's be gone!

(Curtain)

END OF PLAY

Made in the USA
Monee, IL
29 April 2022